The Last Days
according to Jesus

The Last Days according to Jesus

R. C. Sproul

Baker Books

A Division of Baker Book House Co
Grand Rapids, Michigan 49516

To
Garrett Brown

Published by Baker Books
a division of Baker Book House Company
P.O. Box 6287, Grand Rapids, MI 49516-6287

Fourth printing, April 2000

Printed in the United States of America

Library of Congress Cataloging-in-Publication Data

Sproul, R. C. (Robert Charles), 1939–
    The last days according to Jesus / R. C. Sproul.
       p. cm.
    Includes bibliographical references and index.
    ISBN 0-8010-1171-X
    1. Jesus Christ—Prophecies. 2. Second Advent—Biblical teaching. 3. Bible. N.T. Prophecies—Second Advent. I. Title.
BT370.S77 1998
236'.9—dc21   98-30139

For information about academic books, resources for Christian leaders, and all new releases available from Baker Book House, visit our web site:
http://www.bakerbooks.com

For information about Ligonier Ministries and the teaching ministry of R. C. Sproul, visit Ligonier's web site:
http://www.gospelcom.net/ligonier

Contents

List of Tables and Figures

Tables

Figures

You will not have gone through the cities of Israel before the Son of Man comes.

(Matt. 10:23)

Introduction

"Jesus of Nazareth was a false prophet!" This sentiment expresses a view of Christ that goes beyond the borders of slander to flirt with the supreme form of blasphemy from which there is no recovery. It peers into the abyss inhabited by legions of the damned.

Many who shrink from affirming the full deity of Christ hedge their bets by applying the honorific "Prophet" to his name. Few are bold enough in their unbelief to hurl against him the scurrilous epithet "false prophet." In Israel the term *false prophet* signaled a warrant for death by stoning. The false prophet was a scourge to the community precisely because he was guilty of mixing dross with the gold of God's truth, substituting the counterfeit for the genuine, the lie for the truth, and misleading the people of God, sometimes fatally.

The false prophet in Israel was detected by his making future predictions that failed to come to pass. This was the acid test to expose the dreamer who claimed the authority of the divine oracle to sanction erroneous pronouncements. God was enlisted as an ally for disinformation, indeed, claimed as the source or fountain of the poisonous lie. To preface one's declaration with the claim "Thus saith the Lord" was to claim divine inspiration for a mere human opinion, to grasp for infallibility that is not the province of uninspired men.

The charge of false prophecy against Jesus is not made lightly by sober men. The consequences of such calumny are too severe. It takes a brash or supremely confident critic to risk this type of judgment. Such a man was Bertrand Russell. Russell distinguished himself as a world-class philosopher and mathematician. He attained peerage in the British realm for his many accomplishments. He was frequently in the news for his passive resistance to war, particularly nuclear war. Celebrated as one of the leading intellectuals of his era, Russell was taken very seriously by the intelligentsia.

Russell's Rejection of Christ

Russell's little book *Why I Am Not a Christian*[1] set forth his polemic against religion in general and Christianity in particular. He was convinced that religion has had an evil influence on human civilization. "The question of the truth of a religion is one thing, but the question of its usefulness is another," he wrote. "I am as firmly convinced that religions do harm as I am that they are untrue."[2]

Though Russell hedges his bets a little by declaring his general respect for the moral character of Jesus, he does raise objections to Jesus' recorded behavior at certain points. I stress the point of "recorded behavior" because Russell was skeptical regarding the biblical account of the life and teaching of Christ. "Historically it is quite doubtful," he says, "whether Christ ever existed at all, and if He did we do not know anything about Him, so that I am not concerned with the historical question, which is a very difficult one."[3]

Russell continues: "I am concerned with Christ as He appears in the Gospels, taking the Gospel narrative as it stands, and there one does find some things that do not seem to be very wise. For one thing, He certainly thought that His second coming would occur in clouds of glory before the death of all the people who were living at that time."[4]

Russell cites various texts of the New Testament to prove his point: "There are a great many texts that prove that. He says, for instance, 'Ye shall not have gone over the cities of Israel till the Son of Man be come' [Matt. 10:23]. Then He says, 'There are some standing here which shall not taste death till the Son of Man comes into His kingdom' [Matt. 16:28]; and there are a lot of places where it is quite clear that He believed that His second coming would happen during the lifetime of many then living. That was the belief of His earlier followers, and it was the basis of a good deal of His moral teaching. . . . In that respect, clearly He was not so wise as some other people have been, and He was certainly not superlatively wise."[5]

One of Russell's chief criticisms of the Jesus portrayed in the Gospels is that Jesus was wrong with respect to the timing of his future return. At issue for Russell is the time-frame reference of these prophecies. Russell charges that Jesus failed to return during the time frame he had predicted.

There is irony in Russell's negative polemic. One of the most important proofs of Christ's character and the Bible's divine inspiration is Jesus' astonishingly accurate prediction of the destruction of the temple and the fall of Jerusalem, prophecies contained in the Olivet Discourse. There can be little doubt that the biblical record of this prediction antedates the events themselves. It is now almost universally acknowledged that the Gospels of Matthew, Mark, and Luke were written before A.D. 70.

Christ's prophecies in the Olivet Discourse differ sharply from ancient prophecies like those of the Oracle of Delphi, which were exercises in the art of studied ambiguity. They left fulfillment somewhat open ended, and they were capable of disparate interpretation. These oracles are not unlike the predictions found in modern daily horoscopes, which are sufficiently broad or ambiguous to allow for accidental fulfillment.

Nor can Jesus' concrete predictions be attributed to educated guesses or the insight of a futurist. To first-century Jews it was unthinkable that such catastrophic events as the destruction of the Herodian temple, the devastation of the holy city of Jerusalem, and the dispersion of the Jewish people to the four corners of the earth could take place in the foreseeable future. Such events were eminently not foreseeable, save to one who had information from the omniscient God himself.

So the very prophecy that should confirm both the credentials of Jesus and the inspiration of Scripture is, ironically, the prophecy used by critics like Russell to debunk both Jesus and the Bible. Proof for the truth of Scripture and Christ becomes proof for the falsehood of both. As I shall presently endeavor to show, the skepticism expressed by Russell on these matters is by no means limited to him, but is the axe that is ground by a host of higher-critical scholars of the Bible. It would not be an over-statement to suggest that the chief ground for the radical criticism of modern biblical scholarship, which has resulted in a wholesale attack on the trustworthiness of Scripture and a far-reaching skepticism of our ability to know anything about the real historical Jesus, is the thesis that the Gospels' records of Jesus' predictions contain glaring errors and gross inaccuracies.

The main problem with Jesus' predictions in the Olivet Discourse is that they include not only predictions regarding Jerusalem and the temple, which did come to pass with astonishing accuracy, but also predictions of his own coming in glory, or his parousia. It is these predictions regarding Jesus' return on which Russell seized for fodder for his negative *apologia*. It is tempting to dismiss Russell lightly with the charge that, though he was erudite and astute in at least two major academic disciplines, he was not a trained or skilled exegete of Scripture. When he expressed his criticisms of the biblical text, he was speaking outside the field of his expertise. The problem, however, is that Russell's is not a lone voice in recent history. His criticisms are echoed by a multitude of highly learned specialists in the field of biblical studies.

I must include at this point a personal note. My own academic training took place for the most part at institutions of higher learning that are not identified with conservative or evangelical Christianity. One of my chief professors in college was a doctoral student under Rudolf Bultmann. In seminary I was exposed daily to critical theories espoused by my professors regarding the Scripture. What stands out in my memory of those days is the heavy emphasis on biblical texts regarding the return of Christ, which were constantly cited as examples of errors in the New Testament and proof that the text had been edited to accommodate the crisis in the early church caused by the so-called parousia-delay of

Jesus. In a word, much of the criticism leveled against the trust-worthiness of Scripture was linked to questions regarding biblical eschatology.

Jesus' Time-Frame References

The time-frame references of the Olivet Discourse are prominent in the debate over the integrity of both Christ and the Bible. Mark reports this discourse as follows:

> Then as He went out of the temple, one of His disciples said to Him, "Teacher, see what manner of stones and what buildings are here!" And Jesus answered and said to him, "Do you see these great buildings? Not one stone shall be left upon another, that shall not be thrown down."
>
> Now as He sat on the Mount of Olives opposite the temple, Peter, James, John, and Andrew asked Him privately, "Tell us, when will these things be? And what will be the sign when all these things will be fulfilled?" And Jesus, answering them, began to say: "Take heed that no one deceives you. For many will come in My name, saying, 'I am He,' and will deceive many. And when you hear of wars and rumors of wars, do not be troubled; for such things must happen, but the end is not yet. For nation will rise against nation, and kingdom against kingdom. And there will be earthquakes in various places, and there will be famines and troubles. These are the beginnings of sorrows. But watch out for yourselves, for they will deliver you up to councils, and you will be beaten in the synagogues. And you will be brought before rulers and kings for My sake, for a testimony to them. And the gospel must first be preached to all the nations. But when they arrest you and deliver you up, do not worry beforehand, or premeditate what you will speak. But whatever is given you in that hour, speak that; for it is not you who speak, but the Holy Spirit. Now brother will betray brother to death, and a father his child; and children will rise up against parents and cause them to be put to death. And you will be hated by all men for My name's sake. But he who endures to the end shall be saved.
>
> "But when you see the 'abomination of desolation,' spoken of by Daniel the prophet, standing where it ought not" (let the reader

understand), "then let those who are in Judea flee to the mountains. And let him who is on the housetop not go down into the
house, nor enter to take anything out of his house. And let him who
is in the field not go back to get his garment. But woe to those who
are pregnant and to those with nursing babies in those days! And
pray that your flight may not be in winter. For in those days there
will be tribulation, such as has not been from the beginning of creation which God created until this time, nor ever shall be. And
unless the Lord had shortened those days, no flesh would be saved;
but for the elect's sake, whom He chose, He shortened the days.
Then if anyone says to you, 'Look, here is the Christ!' or, 'Look, He
is there!' do not believe it. For false christs and false prophets will
rise and show signs and wonders to deceive, if possible, even the
elect. But take heed; see, I have told you all things beforehand.

"But in those days, after that tribulation, the sun will be darkened,
and the moon will not give its light; the stars of heaven will fall, and
the powers in heaven will be shaken. Then they will see the Son of
Man coming in the clouds with great power and glory. And then He
will send His angels, and gather together His elect from the four
winds, from the farthest part of earth to the farthest part of heaven.

"Now learn this parable from the fig tree: When its branch has
already become tender, and puts forth leaves, you know that summer is near. So you also, when you see these things happening, know
that it is near—at the very doors! Assuredly, I say to you, this generation will by no means pass away till all these things take place. . . ."

(Mark 13:1–30)

The most critical portion of this text is Jesus' declaration that
"this generation will by no means pass away till all these things
take place" (13:30). When Russell pointed to this pronouncement,
he made two important assumptions. The first is that "this generation" refers to a specific time-frame that would be roughly
forty years. That is, the terminus for the fulfillment of this
prophecy is forty years. If Jesus made this announcement sometime between A.D. 30 and 33, then the destruction of Jerusalem
in A.D. 70 would fit perfectly within the time frame. The second
assumption made by Russell (and others) is that the phrase "all
these things" includes all of the subject matter of his future prediction, including his coming in clouds of power and glory.

Given these assumptions, the *prima facie* reading of the text leads to the conclusion that, within the time frame of forty years, not only will the temple and Jerusalem be destroyed, but also the parousia (or coming) of Christ will take place. Since, again according to Russell, the parousia did not take place within this time frame, both Christ and the Bible are wrong.

Both of Russell's assumptions have been challenged in manifold ways, as we will see later. For now, however, we are focusing on the first-glance reading of the text that is held by Russell and others. It is my fear that evangelicals today tend to underplay the significance of the problems inherent in Russell's assumptions. Too often we take a facile approach to the problem that reveals our failure to feel the weight of such objections. This becomes particularly acute when we realize the extent to which these problems have contributed to the entire modern controversy over the inspiration of Scripture and the person and work of Christ. To gain a better feel for the problem, we must take a short reconnaissance of modern views of eschatology.

The Crisis in Eschatology

Though many of the critical views of Scripture prevalent today originated in the Enlightenment, characterized by a reliance on rationalistic and naturalistic philosophy, they did not reach their acme (or nadir) until the development of so-called liberalism that held sway in the nineteenth century. This era was marked by the dominance of Hegelian philosophy, which provided an evolutionary view of history that worked itself out in terms of a dialectical process. As distinguished from the Marxist view of "dialectical materialism," Hegelianism has been dubbed "dialectical idealism."

If there was a buzzword in nineteenth-century theoretical thought, it was the word *evolution*. The idea of evolution was applied not simply to biology, but also to other fields of inquiry. Political theory saw the application of Herbert Spencer's "social Darwinianism," for example. It is important to realize that evolution encompasses chiefly a theory of history whereby not only biological entities undergo a progressive development from the simple to the complex, but also other entities undergo a similar sort of progressive change.

Married to evolutionary philosophy, the Religious Historical School of the nineteenth century considered it axiomatic that all religions go through evolutionary stages of development. They move from the simple to the complex. In this scheme all religions begin with primitive forms of animism and move to a more complex level of sophisticated monotheism. Nineteenth-century scholars such as Julius Wellhausen applied this scheme to the Old Testament. They believed Israelite religion evolved through four distinct stages: animism, polytheism, henotheism, and monotheism (see fig. 0.1).

Animism, the most primitive form, sees objects of nature as being inhabited by evil spirits. Hints of this were seen in the speaking serpent of Genesis 3 and in Abraham's conversing with angels by the Oaks of Mamre. Critics argued that Abraham was having a dialogue with spirits that inhabited the trees.

Polytheism affirms the existence of many gods and goddesses who have designated functions such as those in Roman mythology and the Greek pantheon. Here we find deities of war, wisdom, love, agriculture, and so forth. Polytheism was alleged to exist in the Old Testament, particularly with reference to the "E-Source" of the Pentateuch (the first five books of the Bible), in which the chief name for God was *Elohim*, which has a plural ending.

Henotheism, a transition stage between polytheism and monotheism, is the idea that each nation or ethnic group is ruled by a single god. So there are as many gods as there are nations or ethnic groups. This was alleged to be the case in Israelite religion, which pitted the national god, Yahweh, against the gods of other nations, such as Baal (Judg. 2:11–13) or Dagon (Judg. 16:23).

Finally the idea of monotheism emerged (relatively late in Jewish history), which viewed God as the Lord of all creation.

With the development of nineteenth-century liberalism came a serious effort to modify or revise the essence of biblical religion. Central to this reconstruction of the Christian faith was the attempt to redefine the biblical concept of the kingdom of God.

Fig. 0.1

The Evolution of Israel's Religion
according to the Religious Historical School

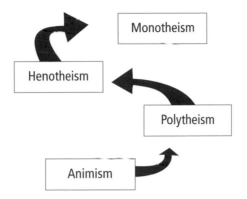

As John Bright has noted in recent times, the motif of God's kingdom weaves together and provides the continuity between the Old and New Testaments. Nineteenth-century liberalism sought a Christian faith that is desupernaturalized and essentially immanentistic in its outlook. Under the influence of Hegelian philosophy, the kingdom of God was evolving naturally without the intrusion of a transcendent God.

Elements of the miraculous were rejected out of hand by thinkers such as David Friedrich Strauss and William Wrede. The miracles of the Bible, especially those attributed to Jesus, were explained in naturalistic terms. For example the feeding of the five thousand was interpreted in various ways, including these two: (1) Jesus and his disciples had a large store of food concealed in a cave. Jesus stood in front of a small opening through which provisions were secretly passed to him by his hidden disciples, and were then distributed to the multitudes. This crass view reduced Jesus to a clever magician and a charlatan. (2) Jesus used the example of the lad who had offered to Jesus his meager provisions, to exhort those who had brought lunches to share with those who had not. Thus this was not a miracle of nature but an "ethical" miracle, persuading those who had much, to share with those who had nothing.

The accent on ethics was primary to the liberal revision of biblical Christianity. Leading thinkers such as Albrecht Ritschl eschewed the influence of Greek metaphysical thought on the formulation of historic creeds such as attributing the equality of divine essence to members of the Trinity. He saw the essence of Jesus' teaching not as supernatural redemption but as ethical and moral values. Liberal scholars recast Jesus as the supreme teacher of ethics rather than as the incarnate Son of God who was born of a virgin, who died an atoning death of cosmic significance, and who was raised bodily from the dead and ascended into heaven. These supernatural elements of the biblical portrait were rejected, and in their place was substituted the moralist Jew who advocated a kingdom of values and social responsibility.

It was somewhat fashionable in the nineteenth century to compare the world religions in an effort to discern and distill the essence of them all into a basic common denominator. Here Christianity suffered from reductionism with a vengeance. Church historian Adolf Harnack published a little book on the *Wesen,* the "essence" or "being," of Christianity, which was published in English as *What Is Christianity?*[6] In this volume Harnack reduced the essence of Christianity to two foundational concepts: the universal fatherhood of God and the universal brotherhood of man.

Schweitzer's Quest

Against this backdrop of liberalism, Albert Schweitzer wrote his watershed book, *The Quest of the Historical Jesus,*[7] which appeared first in 1906 under the German title *Von Reimarus zu Wrede* ("From Reimarus to Wrede"). As the German title suggests, Schweitzer gave a critical analysis of developments in nineteenth-century thought. He embraced much of the thought of Johannes Weiss, who had attacked Ritschl's concept of an ethical-value kingdom that is totally immanent and evolutionary. Weiss argued that this concept is rooted not in the New Testament but in Enlightenment theology and the ethical philosophy of Immanuel Kant.

Herman Ridderbos says of Weiss: ". . . [He] argued that Jesus' preaching of the kingdom of God can only be understood in the light of and against the background of the world of thought of his time, especially of the late Jewish apocalyptic writings. On this view, every conception of the kingdom of God as an immanent community in course of development or as an ethical ideal is consequently to be rejected; for it becomes clear that the kingdom of God is a purely future and eschatological event, presupposing the end of this world; and, therefore, cannot possibly reveal itself already in this world."[8]

When Weiss speaks of the kingdom's eschatological character, he uses the word *eschatological* to mean more than "the future" or "the last things." Here the term carries the idea of "an action wrought by God that is transcendent and catastrophic." It is not a future event that emerges through evolutionary development, but a future event that is brought on suddenly from above, an intrusion of the work of God.

This eschatological concept of the kingdom of God was embraced by Schweitzer. He saw this as the key to understanding the life and teaching of Jesus. Schweitzer called this view "consistent eschatology." Though he sought to interpret the life of Jesus against the backdrop of a transcendent eschatology, he concluded that Jesus' own eschatological expectations had been unfulfilled. The historical Jesus believed that the kingdom would be inaugurated by a catastrophic act of God, but this divine act did not materialize.

According to Schweitzer, Jesus underwent a series of crises. He expected the dramatic coming of the kingdom at different points of his ministry, such as when he sent out the seventy. Jesus had to face postponements to his expectation. He finally hoped that his submission to the cross would provoke God to act. When that also failed to happen, Jesus cried out in despair, "My God, My God, why have You forsaken Me?" (Matt. 27:46). This was the anguished cry of a disillusioned man.

For Schweitzer, the eschatology of Jesus was unrealized. This led to Schweitzer's concept of "parousia-delay." The writings of the apostolic church reflect an adjustment in thinking, a movement from an expectation of Christ's imminent return (and the consummation of the kingdom) to an expectation of his delayed return in the unknown future.

Though Schweitzer rejected the concept of an ethical kingdom as the motif of Jesus' teaching and self-consciousness and replaced it with an eschatological view, it was an eschatology that remained unrealized. Though his view did not prevail among scholars, Schweitzer's work provoked many theories that wrestled with the problems he had raised.

Schweitzer's work was followed by that of C. H. Dodd, who introduced a full-scale system of "realized eschatology." For Dodd the eschatological kingdom of God is ushered in during the ministry of Christ. The presence of the kingdom is a common theme in Jesus' parables, as Dodd notes in *The Parables of the Kingdom*.[9] In another work Dodd says:

> The eschatology of the early Church has two sides. On the one hand we have the belief that with the coming of Christ the "fulness of time" has arrived, the prophecies are fulfilled, and the Kingdom of God is inaugurated on earth. On the other hand we have the expectation of a consummation still pending in the future. There is some tension between the two in almost all New Testament writings. They differ among themselves with respect to the relation conceived to exist between the fulfillment which is already [a] matter of history, and the fulfilment which belongs to the future. In the Fourth Gospel the language of "futurist eschatology" is little used.[10]

For Dodd the kingdom is essentially a spiritual reality that has been completely realized in the past. The tension between realized and unrealized eschatology has plagued New Testament scholars in our time. Attempts to relieve this stress have been offered by both Oscar Cullmann and Herman Ridderbos. Both scholars have sought to understand the New Testament concept of the kingdom of God in terms of the present and the future.

Ridderbos has popularized the concept of the "already" and the "not yet" of the kingdom (the *als* and the *nog niet*). When John the Baptist appears on the stage of history, a moment of crisis is reached. Unlike the Old Testament prophets, who announced the coming of the kingdom in the unknown or distant future, John announces that its arrival is imminent. He is the herald of the coming kingdom. John declares that "the ax is laid to the root of the trees" and "His winnowing fan is in His hand" (Matt. 3:10, 12). The images of the axe and the fan both call attention to the radical nearness of the kingdom.

The image of the axe does not indicate that the woodsman is merely thinking about cutting down a tree or that he has merely begun the task by striking at the outer bark. The image instead is that the task is nearly complete. The axe has already penetrated to the core of the tree, hinting that one more decisive stroke will make it fall.

The fan refers to the winnowing fork used by a farmer to separate the wheat from the chaff. The farmer is not heading to his barn to get the fan. It is already in his hand and he is about to begin winnowing.

The radical character of John's baptism is also seen in this light. He called Jewish people to undergo this cleansing rite because their King is about to appear and they are defiled and unready to meet him. Consequently John calls the people to repent and be baptized. "The kingdom of heaven is *at hand*" (Matt. 3:2). With the coming of Jesus, the kingdom is inaugurated, reaching its New Testament acme in his ascension. The ascension is not merely a "going up" to heaven. It is a going up for a specific event, his coronation and investiture as the King of Kings and Lord of Lords. Insofar as Jesus presently occupies this seat of cosmic authority, the kingdom of God has come. Yet his reign remains invisible to men. It is yet to be made fully manifest on earth.

At this point Oscar Cullmann introduces his famous D-Day analogy. The resurrection and ascension of Christ represents the D-day of the kingdom, the decisive turning point in redemptive history. In World War II D-Day was not the end of the war, but it was such a decisive turning point that for all intents and purposes the war was over. What was left was a mop-up exercise (the Battle of the Bulge notwithstanding). In like manner the decisive work of the kingdom has been accomplished. We are living in the interim awaiting the consummation that will occur at Christ's parousia.

In addition to these views of the kingdom and eschatology, we encounter modern Dispensationalism, which regards the king-

Preterism	
Preterism	The Kingdom is a present reality
Radical preterism	All future prophecies in the NT have already been fulfilled.
Moderate preterism	Many future prophecies in the NT have already been fulfilled. Some crucial prophecies have not yet been fulfilled.

dom as future. For Dispensationalism the kingdom will not come until the parousia. Likewise, various forms of preterism have emerged. Preterists argue not only that the kingdom is a present reality, but also that in a real historical sense the parousia has already occurred.

Moderate Preterism

We may distinguish between two distinct forms of preterism, which I call radical preterism and moderate preterism. Radical preterism sees all future prophecies of the New Testament as having already taken place, while moderate preterism still looks to the future for crucial events to occur. The purpose of this book is to evaluate moderate preterism and its view of eschatology.

Perhaps the most important scholar of the preterist school is J. Stuart Russell. Russell's book *The Parousia*[11] first appeared in 1878, with a second edition following nine years later. The 1887 edition was reprinted in 1983. Russell anticipated many of the theories that would be presented by twentieth-century scholars. His chief concern was the time-frame references of New Testament eschatology, particularly with respect to Jesus' utterances concerning the coming of the kingdom and to Jesus' Olivet Discourse. In his summary at the end of the book, Russell writes:

> Without going over the ground already traversed it may suffice here to appeal to three distinct and decisive declarations of our Lord respecting the time of His coming, each of them accompanied with a solemn affirmation:
>
> 1. "Verily I say unto you, Ye shall not have gone over the cities of Israel, till the Son of man be come" (Matt. 10:23).

2. "Verily I say unto you, There be some standing here, which shall not taste death, till they see the Son of man coming in his kingdom" (Matt. 16:28).

3. "Verily I say unto you, This generation shall not pass, till all these things be fulfilled" (Matt. 24:34).

The plain grammatical meaning of these statements has been fully discussed in these pages. No violence can extort from them any other sense than the obvious and unambiguous one, viz. that our Lord's second coming would take place within the limits of the existing generation.[12]

The central thesis of Russell and indeed of all preterists is that the New Testament's time-frame references with respect to the parousia point to a fulfillment within the lifetime of at least some of Jesus' disciples. Some hold to a primary fulfillment in

The Life of James Stuart Russell	
1816	Born on November 28 in Elgin, Morayshire.
1829	Entered King's College, Aberdeen.
1835	Received M.A. degree.
1843	Became assistant minister in Congregational church in Great Yarmouth. Later became the minister.
1843	Attended the founding of the Evangelical Alliance.
1857	Became minister in Congregational church in Tottenham and Edmonton.
1862	Became minister in Congregational church in Bayswater.
1878	Published *The Parousia* anonymously.
1887	Published second edition of *The Parousia* under his name.
1888	Retired from the ministry.
1895	Died on October 5.

A.D. 70, with a secondary and final fulfillment in the yet-unknown future. Whatever else may be said of preterism, it has achieved at least two things: (1) It has focused attention on the time-frame references of New Testament eschatology, and (2) it has highlighted the significance of Jerusalem's destruction in redemptive history.

Contemporary eschatological theories, especially those found within evangelicalism, are keenly interested in the significance of events surrounding modern Israel and the city of Jerusalem. Karl

Barth once remarked that the modern Christian must read with the Bible in one hand and the newspaper in the other. The dramatic return to Palestine of the Jews, the creation of the state of Israel in 1948, and the recapture of Jerusalem in 1967 have provoked a frenzy of interest in eschatology. The question persists: What is the significance of modern Israel and Jerusalem to biblical prophecy?

Whatever one's view of modern Jerusalem, it is essential that we examine the significance of its destruction by the Romans in the first century. If the reconstruction of Jerusalem is significant, it can only be so in light of its earlier destruction. No matter what view of eschatology we embrace, we must take seriously the redemptive-historical importance of Jerusalem's destruction in A.D. 70.

In *The Last Days according to Jesus* we will devote considerable attention to New Testament prophecies bearing on the destruction of Jerusalem, as well as the eyewitness account of it provided by Jewish historian Flavius Josephus.

Prophecies of the coming of God's kingdom and the parousia of Christ are linked biblically with prophecies of the day of the Lord. This day is viewed to some degree as a day of divine judgment and the pouring out of God's wrath. These concepts are interconnected and must be viewed in relation to each other.

From the Enlightenment onward, the church has been gripped by a severe crisis regarding the trustworthiness of Scripture. The spirit of skepticism that reigns in so many quarters is a direct result of the avalanche of criticism leveled against the Bible. Early in this century Dutch theologian Abraham Kuyper lamented that biblical criticism had degenerated into biblical vandalism. The task in our time is to answer the critics who have scorned the Scriptures and given us a Christ of their own imaginations. The only Christ is the biblical Christ. All revisionist Christs are but shadows of the antichrist.

Due to the crisis in confidence in the truth and authority of Scripture and the subsequent crisis regarding the real historical Jesus, eschatology must come to grips with the tensions of time-frame references in the New Testament.

*Then the sign of the Son of Man
will appear in heaven,
and then all the tribes
of the earth . . .
will see the Son of Man
coming on the clouds of heaven. . . .*

(Matt. 24:30)

What Did Jesus Teach on Mount Olivet?

he Olivet Discourse takes its name from the place where Jesus delivered it. This discourse is recorded in all three Synoptic Gospels: Matthew (chapter 24), Mark (chapter 13), and Luke (chapter 21). This is the longest teaching discourse recorded in the Gospel of Mark. "In the Gospel of Mark there is no passage more problematic than the prophetic discourse of Jesus on the destruction of the Temple," says William L. Lane. "The questions posed by the form and content of the chapter and by its relationship to the Gospel as a whole are complex and difficult and have been the occasion of an extensive literature."[1] What Lane says of Mark could also be said of Matthew and Luke.

Biblical scholars have questioned the authenticity of the discourse, which has been called "the small apocalypse." Vincent Taylor cites this theory, which has been adopted by many critical scholars: "The suggestion is that, in anticipation of the horrors of the siege of Jerusalem, some unknown Christian edited a small Jewish or Jewish-Christian apocalypse as a kind of fly-sheet to give encouragement and hope to the Christians of his day, and incorporated therewith eschatological sayings of Jesus."[2]

Other theories have claimed that the discourse is either completely inauthentic or reflects the work of a later redactor ("editor"), who fused together different strands of an oral tradition that originated in the teaching of Jesus, but not in the homogeneous form found in the Gospels themselves.

The discourse begins with these words:

Matthew 24:1–2	Mark 13:1–2	Luke 21:5–6
Then Jesus went out and departed from the temple, and His disciples came to Him to show Him the buildings of the temple.	Then as He went out of the temple, one of His disciples	Then, as some
	said to Him,	spoke of the temple, how it was adorned
	"Teacher, see what manner of stones and what buildings are here!"	with beautiful stones
And Jesus	And Jesus answered and	and donations, He
said to them,	said to him,	said, "As for these things which
"Do you not see all these things? Assuredly, I say to you,	"Do you see these great buildings?	you see,
		the days will come in which
not one stone shall be left here upon another, that shall not be thrown down."	Not one stone shall be left upon another, that shall not be thrown down."	not one stone shall be left upon another that shall not be thrown down."

Jesus begins the Olivet Discourse with a statement about every stone of the temple being "thrown down." It is important to note that the entire discourse is provoked by his words about the destruction of the temple. The disciples respond to his prediction by asking about the time-frame for this event.

Matthew 24:3	Mark 13:3–4	Luke 21:7
Now as He sat on the Mount of Olives,	Now as He sat on the Mount of Olives opposite the temple,	
the disciples	Peter, James, John, and Andrew	And they
came to Him privately, saying,	asked Him privately,	asked Him, saying, "Teacher,
"Tell us, when will these things be? And what will be the sign of Your coming, and of the end of the age?"	"Tell us, when will these things be? And what will be the sign	but when will these things be? And what sign
	when all these things will be fulfilled?"	will there be when these things are about to take place?"

In all three Gospels the disciples ask two questions: (1) When will these things be? (2) What will be the sign of their fulfillment? We notice, however, that only one of the three accounts includes the question about the coming of Christ and the end of the age. This question is reported by Matthew but omitted by both Luke and Mark.

In his *Commentary on a Harmony of the Evangelists* John Calvin says that what is explicit in Matthew is implicit in Mark and Luke:

Mark mentions four disciples, *Peter, James, John, and Andrew.* But neither he nor Luke states the matter so fully as Matthew; for they

---

Questions Jesus Answered on Mount Olivet

Question 1	When will these things be?
Question 2	What will be the sign of a) your coming and b) the end of the age?

only say that the disciples inquired about the time of the destruction of *the temple,* and—as it was a thing difficult to be believed—what outward *sign* of it God would give from heaven. Matthew tells us that they inquired about the time *of Christ's coming, and of the end of the world.* But it must be observed that, having believed from their infancy that the temple would stand till the end of time, and having this opinion deeply rooted in their minds, they did not suppose that, while the building *of the world* stood, the *temple* could fall to ruins. Accordingly, as soon as Christ said that *the temple* would be destroyed, their thoughts immediately turned to *the end of the world....* They associate *the coming of Christ* and *the end of the world* as things inseparable from each other....[3]

Calvin regarded as erroneous the disciples' assumption that the destruction of Jerusalem would coincide with the coming of Christ and the end of the world. This means that Jesus was answering a question that contained false assumptions.

The preterist view of J. Stuart Russell differs sharply from the view of Calvin. Russell argues that the disciples' assumption was correct—with one crucial qualifier: the disciples were asking not about the end of the world, but about the end of the age. This distinction is critical not only to Russell, but to virtually all preterists. The end in view is not the end of all time but the end of the Jewish age.

"It is generally assumed," Russell writes, "that the disciples came to our Lord with three different questions, relating to different events separated from each other by a long interval of time; that the first inquiry, 'When shall *these things* be?'—had reference to the approaching destruction of the temple; that the second and third questions, 'What shall be the sign of *thy coming,* and of the *end of the world?*'—referred to events long posterior to the destruction of Jerusalem, and, in fact, not yet accomplished."[4]

Russell voices his dissent by arguing that all three Gospel writers correctly incorporate all three things within the same general historical event: "St. Mark and St. Luke make the question of the disciples refer to *one* event and *one* time. . . . It is not only presumable, therefore, but indubitable, that the questions of the disciples only refer to *different aspects of the same great event.* This harmonises the statements of St. Matthew with those of the other Evangelists, and is plainly required by the circumstances of the case."[5]

Clearly Russell assumes that the text of Scripture is inspired, and he approaches the question of harmonizing the Gospel accounts of the Olivet Discourse on that basis. Given the trustworthiness of the Bible, it becomes clear that if all three events are merely implicit in the disciples' query in Mark and Luke, these events are tied together explicitly in the Gospel of Matthew. The disciples' unambiguous question is a time-frame question. The disciples ask *when* these things will come to pass and what is the *sign* of Christ's coming and of the *end?*

> **Books by James Stuart Russell**
>
> *A Leaf from the Early History of the Ancient Congregational Church in Great Yarmouth, 1642–1670.* Yarmouth, 1850.
> *Nonconformity in the Seventeenth Century: An Historical Discourse Delivered at the Celebration of the Bicentenary of the Congregational Church, Wattisfield, Suffolk . . . With an Outline of the History of the Church by Its Pastor [W. Warren].* Norwich, 1854.
> *The Parousia: A Critical Inquiry into the New Testament Doctrine of Our Lord's Second Coming.* London: Daldy, Isbister & Co., 1878.
> *The Parousia: A Critical Inquiry into the New Testament Doctrine of Our Lord's Second Coming.* New ed. London: T. Fisher Unwin, 1887.

A Solemn Warning

Jesus begins his answer with a solemn warning against deception. Matthew records his answer as follows:

And Jesus answered and said to them: "Take heed that no one deceives you. "For many will come in My name, saying, 'I am the

Christ,' and will deceive many. And you will hear of wars and rumors of wars. See that you are not troubled; for all these things must come to pass, but the end is not yet. For nation will rise against nation, and kingdom against kingdom. And there will be famines, pestilences, and earthquakes in various places. All these are the beginning of sorrows. Then they will deliver you up to tribulation and kill you, and you will be hated by all nations for My name's sake. And then many will be offended, will betray one another, and will hate one another. Then many false prophets will rise up and deceive many. And because lawlessness will abound, the love of many will grow cold. But he who endures to the end shall be saved."

(Matt. 24:4–13)

Jesus focuses initially on the perils posed by the appearance of false messiahs. Russell argues that the deceptive claims of these false messiahs were fulfilled in the period between the ascension of Christ and the destruction of Jerusalem: "False Christs and false prophets began to make their appearance at a very early period of the Christian era, and continued to infest the land down to the very close of Jewish history. In the procuratorship of [Pontius] Pilate (A.D. 36), one such appeared in Samaria, and deluded great multitudes. There was another in the procuratorship of Cuspius Fadus (A.D. 45). During the government of Felix (A.D. 53–60), [Flavius] Josephus tells us 'the country was full of robbers, magicians, false prophets, false Messiahs, and impostors, who deluded the people with promises of great events.'"[6]

Calvin agreed that a rash of false messiahs arose in the early-church era. "For shortly after Christ's resurrection, there arose impostors, every one of whom professed to be *the Christ*," Calvin writes. "And as the true Redeemer had not only been removed from the world, but oppressed by the ignominy of the cross, and yet the minds of all were excited by the hope and inflamed with the desire of redemption, those men had in their power a plausible opportunity of deceiving. Nor can it be doubted, that God permitted such reveries to impose on the Jews, who had so basely rejected his Son."[7]

Table 1.1

**Signs of Jesus' Coming
and of the End**

	Matt. 24:	Mark 13:	Luke 21:
False christs	5	6	8
Wars and rumors of wars	6	7	9
between nations and	7	8	10
between kingdoms	7	8	10
Famines	7	8	11
Pestilences, troubles	7	8	11
Earthquakes	7	8	11
Persecution of Christ's disciples	9–10	9, 11–13	12–17
Apostasy of professing Christians	10		
False prophets	11		
Lawlessness	12		
Gospel preaching worldwide	14	10	
Abomination of desolation	15	14	20
Great tribulation, distress	21	19	23
Astronomical phenomena	29	24–25	25

Though Calvin acknowledged that the problem of false christs plagued the early church after the resurrection of Christ, he applied the warning to the church of all ages, not limiting it to the church of the first century. This application is quite legitimate, as the appearance of impostors is a perennial problem. The question, however, is this: What significance did Jesus' warning have for and to his immediate hearers? It is one thing for us to ask how Jesus' teaching applies to us; it is quite another to ask what it meant in its original context. We must keep in mind that Jesus was answering questions posed by his disciples, questions about *when* his previous utterances would be fulfilled. His words were directed to them. "Take heed," he said, "that no one deceives *you*." He told his disciples that they would hear of wars and rumors of wars, and so forth.

The calamities Jesus enumerates, including famines, pestilences, earthquakes, and wars, are described as "the beginning of sorrows." Immediately following this he said that the disciples *(you)* would be delivered up to affliction, to be hated and killed. Again the preterist view of Russell links these calamities to events that actually took place in the interim between Christ's resurrection and Jerusalem's destruction.

> . . . In Alexandria, in Seleucia, in Syria, in Babylonia, there were violent tumults between the Jews and the Greeks, the Jews and the Syrians, inhabiting the same cities. . . . In the reign of Caligula great apprehensions were entertained in Judea of war with the Romans, in consequence of that tyrant's proposal to place his statue in the temple. In the reign of the Emperor Claudius (A.D. 41–54), there were four seasons of great scarcity. In the fourth year of his reign, the famine in Judea was so severe, that the price of food became enormous and great numbers perished. Earthquakes occurred in each of the reigns of Caligula and Claudius.
>
> Such calamities, the Lord gave His disciples to understand, would precede the "end." But they were not its immediate antecedents. They were the "beginning of the end"; but "*the* end is not yet."[8]

Jesus described these events as "the beginning of sufferings." W. F. Albright and C. S. Mann comment on this phrase: "Literally, the 'beginnings of birth-pains,' an almost technical term for the sufferings which would immediately precede a new age. . . . The age of the Messiah's reign, seen in the context of the upheavals which surrounded the spread of the community, was certainly ushered in with much suffering."[9]

In similar fashion William L. Lane notes: "To express this fact Jesus used a phrase which became technical in rabbinic literature to describe the period of intense suffering preceding messianic deliverance, 'the birthpangs (of the Messiah).' In the Old Testament the pangs of birth are a recurring image of divine judgment. . . ."[10]

They are mentioned in the context of his answer to the disciples' question concerning when Jesus' prophecies would be fulfilled. Russell argues correctly that these are precursors of fulfillment, things that will happen before Jesus' words are fulfilled. If this prophecy includes the prediction of Jerusalem's destruction, then the natural meaning of his words is that these things must take place before Jerusalem and the temple are destroyed.

Perhaps the most crucial question regarding Jesus' words is this: What does Jesus mean by *the end?* The end of what? Is Jesus speaking of the end of the temple? The end of the world? The end of the age? Is he speaking of the end of *one* of these things? *Some* of these things? Or *all* the things incorporated in his prophecy?

A Witness to All Nations

Matthew then reports more of the discourse: "And this gospel of the kingdom will be preached in all the world as a witness to all the nations, and then the end will come" (Matt. 24:14).

Jesus cites another phenomenon that must take place before "the end" comes: The gospel will be preached in all the world. This "sign" is widely regarded today as being unfulfilled, as there remain remote tribes and peoples who have not yet heard the gospel.

Russell argues, however, that this precursor to the end was already accomplished in apostolic times: "One other 'sign' was to precede and usher in the consummation," writes Russell. "'The gospel of the kingdom shall be preached in all the world *(oi-koumenē)* for a witness unto all nations: and then shall the end come.' We have already adverted [or alluded] to the fulfilment of this prediction within the apostolic age. We have the authority of St. Paul for such a universal diffusion of the gospel in his days as to verify the saying of our Lord. (See Col. 1:6, 23.) But for this explicit testimony from an apostle it would have been impossible to persuade some expositors that our Lord's words had been in any sense fulfilled previous to the destruction of Jerusalem."[11]

The passage in question reads as follows: "[The gospel] has come to you, as it has also in all the world, and is bringing forth fruit, as it is also among you since the day you heard and knew the grace of God in truth. . . . if indeed you continue in the faith, grounded and steadfast, and are not moved away from the hope of the gospel which you heard, which was preached to every creature under heaven, of which I, Paul, became a minister" (Col. 1:6, 23).

Russell links this statement with Jesus' earlier prediction:

> Here it may be proper to call to mind the note of time, given on a previous occasion to the disciples as indicative of our Lord's coming: "Verily I say unto you, Ye shall not have gone over the cities of Israel, till the Son of man be come" (Matt. 10:23). Comparing this declaration with the prediction before us (Matt. 24:14), we may see the perfect consistency of the two statements, and also the *"terminus ad quem"* in both. In the one case it is the evangelisation of the land of Israel, in the other, the evangelisation of the Roman empire that is referred to as the precursor of the Parousia. Both statements are true. . . . The wide diffusion of the gospel, both in the land of Israel and throughout the Roman empire, is sufficient to justify the prediction of our Lord.[12]

Though Russell links this coming of the Son of Man with the parousia, other scholars, such as Albright and Mann, see it as being fulfilled with the resurrection of Christ, divorcing it from the second coming, or parousia, of Jesus.

The Abomination of Desolation

The following section of the Olivet Discourse concerns the manifestation of the abomination of desolation:

> "Therefore when you see the 'abomination of desolation,' spoken of by Daniel the prophet, standing in the holy place" (whoever reads, let him understand), "then let those who are in Judea flee to the mountains. Let him who is on the housetop not come down to take anything out of his house. And let him who is in the field not go back to get his clothes. But woe to those who are pregnant and to those with nursing babies in those days! And pray that your flight may not be in winter or on the Sabbath. For then there will be great tribulation, such as has not been since the beginning of

the world until this time, no, nor ever shall be. And unless those days were shortened, no flesh would be saved; but for the elect's sake those days will be shortened."

(Matt. 24:15–22)

This segment of the discourse is widely understood today to refer to an event that has not yet transpired, an event popularly described as the great tribulation. It has given rise to a multitude of interpretations, particularly within dispensational theology regarding the time of the rapture, whether it is before the tribulation, in the middle of it, or after it. We will examine the question of the rapture later. For the present we merely note in passing that a host of controversial eschatological theories come into play with respect to this text.

The preterist view includes the tribulation and the abomination of desolation with signs that take place prior to the destruction of Jerusalem. "No argument is required to prove the strict and exclusive reference of this section to Jerusalem and Judea," Russell contends. "Here we can detect no trace of a double meaning, of primary and ulterior fulfilments, of underlying and typical senses. Everything is national, local, and near: '*the land*' is the land of Judea—'*this people*' is the people of Israel—and the '*time*' the lifetime of the disciples—'*When* YE *therefore shall see.*'"[13]

Russell goes on to argue for a first-century fulfillment of this prophecy: "Most expositors find an allusion to the standards of the Roman legions in the expression, 'the abomination of desolation,' and the explanation is highly probable. The eagles were the objects of religious worship to the soldiers; and the parallel passage in St. Luke is all but conclusive evidence that this is the true meaning. We know from Josephus that the attempt of a Roman general (Vitellius), in the reign of Tiberius, to march his troops through Judea was resisted by the Jewish authorities, on the ground that the idolatrous images on their ensigns would be a profanation of the law."[14]

Albright and Mann provide the following note to the text of Matthew 24:15:

Matthew's tradition here makes explicit what is only hinted at in Mark, who does not mention the prophetic oracle. In addition, Matthew speaks of the *holy place* and so emphatically refers to the temple. The quotation is from Dan. 9:27. Cf. the idol altar of 1 Macc. 1:54, 59. With the example of Antiochus Epiphanes in mind, Jesus required neither prescience nor unusual insight to see where the rise of nationalism under Roman occupation would lead. Whether the *abominable sacrilege* refers to actual idolatry, or to the entrance of Roman imperial-eagle standards into the temple area, is immaterial. It was common practice then and for long centuries before, to assert sovereignty over a nation by dethroning its gods and replacing them by those of the conqueror.[15]

John Calvin writes concerning this passage:

Because the destruction of the temple and city of Jerusalem, together with the overthrow of the whole Jewish government, was (as we have already said) a thing incredible, and because it might be thought strange, that the disciples could not be saved without being torn from that nation, to which had been committed *the adoption and the covenant* (Rom. 9:4) of eternal salvation, Christ confirms both by the testimony of *Daniel.* As if he had said, That you may not be too strongly attached to the temple and to the ceremonies of the Law, God has limited them to a fixed time, and has long ago declared, that when the Redeemer should come, sacrifices would cease; and that it may not give you uneasiness to be cut off from your own nation, God has also forewarned his people, that in due time it would be rejected.[16]

Russell then comments on the following portion of Matthew's text:

"Then if anyone says to you, 'Look, here is the Christ!' or 'There!' do not believe it. For false christs and false prophets will arise and show great signs and wonders, so as to deceive, if possible, even the elect. See, I have told you beforehand. Therefore if they say to you, 'Look, He is in the desert!' do not go out; or 'Look, He is in the inner rooms!' do not believe it. For as the lightning comes from the east and flashes to the west, so also will the coming of the Son of Man be. For wherever the carcass is, there the eagles will be gathered together."

(Matt. 24:23–28)

Russell maintains that the text follows in unbroken continuity from what has preceded it.

> The very first word is indicative of continuity—"Then" *[tote]*; and every succeeding word is plainly addressed to the disciples themselves, for their personal warning and guidance. It is clear that our Lord gives them intimation of what would shortly come to pass, or at least what they might live to witness with their own eyes. It is a vivid representation of what actually occurred in the last days of the Jewish commonwealth. . . . The Jewish historian [Josephus] states: "Of so great a multitude, not one escaped. Their destruction was caused by a false prophet, who had on that day proclaimed to those remaining in the city, that 'God commanded them to go up to the temple, there to receive the signs of their deliverance.'"[17]

Russell argues that the carcass where the eagles will be gathered refers to the guilty and devoted children of Israel who will be destroyed by the Roman legions. The carcass is Israel, and the eagles are Rome.

The Appearing of the Son

Crucial to Russell's view is the link between Matthew 24:28 and the following verses that describe the signs of the appearing of the Son of Man in clouds of glory:

> "Immediately after the tribulation of those days the sun will be darkened, and the moon will not give its light; the stars will fall from heaven, and the powers of the heavens will be shaken. Then the sign of the Son of Man will appear in heaven, and then all the tribes of the earth will mourn, and they will see the Son of Man coming on the clouds of heaven with power and great glory. And

He will send His angels with a great sound of a trumpet, and they will gather together His elect from the four winds, from one end of heaven to the other."

(Matt. 24:29–31)

This passage describes the parousia in vivid and graphic images of astronomical perturbations. It speaks of signs in the sky that will be visible and the sound of a trumpet that will be audible. Perhaps no portion of the Olivet Discourse provides more difficulties to the preterist view than this one. This portion leads many interpreters to see a clear historical division between references to the destruction of Jerusalem and references to the parousia of Christ. These interpreters grant that the destruction of the temple and Jerusalem took place within the time-frame of one generation, but insist that Christ has yet to appear in clouds of glory. This is true of interpreters from both the liberal and the conservative ends of the theological spectrum. For the preterism of Russell and others to work, they must give a credible explanation for how these verses fit into the time-frame of the first century.

Because Matthew 24:29–31 begins with the adverb *immediately*, Russell insists that this links the tribulation (in Matt. 24:15–22) to a near-at-hand manifestation of Christ in glory. Russell sees no possibility of any great interval of time between these two events. To argue that the second event occurred in the first century, Russell must demonstrate that the tribulation refers to the calamity suffered by the Jews during the destruction of Jerusalem.

Russell says:

But the scene of the "great tribulation" is undeniably Jerusalem and Judea (vv. 15, 16); so that no break in the subject of the discourse is allowable. Again, in ver. 30, we read that "*all the tribes of the land [pasai ai phulai tēs gēs]* shall mourn," referring evidently to the population of the land of Judea; and nothing can be more forced and unnatural than to make it include, as [John Peter] Lange does, "all the races and peoples" of the globe. The restricted sense of the word *gē* [= land] in the New Testament is common; and when connected, as it is here, with the word "*tribes*" *[phulai]*, its limitation to the land of Israel is obvious. This is the view adopted by Dr. [George] Campbell and Moses Stuart, and it is indeed self-evident.[18]

Many commentators strongly disagree with this assessment of the text. To them the meaning of the reference is not so self-evident. Calvin, for example, said that "*the tribulation of those days* is improperly interpreted by some commentators to mean the destruction of Jerusalem."[19] Others, such as A. W. Argyle, see the connection between this text and the text of Zechariah 12:10 but give it a wider meaning than the tribes of Israel.[20]

The graphic imagery of the events accompanying the parousia function as the chief reason why many, if not most, commentators view this segment of the discourse as being not yet fulfilled. Russell was well aware of this.

> But, it is answered, the character of our Lord's language in this passage necessitates its application to a grand and awful catastrophe which is still future, and can be properly understood of nothing less than the total dissolution of the fabric of the universe, and the end of all things. How can any one pretend, it is said, that the sun has been darkened, that the moon has withdrawn her light, that the stars have fallen from heaven, that the Son of man has been seen coming in the clouds of heaven with power and great glory? Did such phenomena occur at the destruction of Jerusalem, or can they apply to anything else than the final consummation of all things?[21]

The questions Russell anticipates are exacerbated when one considers other New Testament texts that refer to the parousia of Christ. One such text is found in the Book of Acts: "Now when He had spoken these things, while they watched, He was taken up, and a cloud received Him out of their sight. And while they looked steadfastly toward heaven as He went up, behold, two men stood by them in white apparel, who also said, 'Men of Galilee, why do you stand gazing up into heaven? This same Jesus, who was taken up from you into heaven, will so come in like manner as you saw Him go into heaven.'" (Acts 1:9–11)

Luke's record of the ascension of Christ makes it clear that for the disciples present it was a visual experience. They *watched*

Christ as he was taken up in the cloud. They remained transfixed by the sight, gazing up into heaven. When the angels appeared, they declared that Jesus would come *in like manner* as he had departed from them. This would seem to indicate that, if his departure in the glory cloud was visible, then his return in the glory cloud would also be visible. Christ's ascension cannot be regarded as a spiritual or mystical vision without doing radical violence to the text.

Russell responds by appealing to the literary nature of prophecy.

> ... Symbol and metaphor belong to the grammar of prophecy, as every reader of the Old Testament prophets must know. Is it not reasonable that the doom of Jerusalem should be depicted in language as glowing and rhetorical as the destruction of Babylon, or Bozrah, or Tyre? How then does the prophet Isaiah describe the downfall of Babylon?
>
> "Behold the day of the Lord cometh, cruel both with wrath and fierce anger, to lay the land desolate: and he shall destroy the sinners thereof out of it. *For the stars of heaven and the constellations thereof shall not give their light: the sun shall be darkened in his going forth, and the moon shall not cause her light to shine. . . . I will shake the heavens, and the earth shall remove out of her place"* (Isaiah 13:9, 10, 13).[22]

The imagery employed by Isaiah is striking in its parallel to that of the language used by Jesus in the Olivet Discourse. This is one of the strongest points of Russell's argument. He continues by citing other Old Testament passages that employ the same type of imagery:

> ... The prophet Isaiah announces the desolation of Bozrah, the capital of Edom, in the following language: "*The mountains shall be melted with the blood of the slain. . . . All the host of heaven shall be dissolved, and the heavens shall be rolled together as a scroll: and all their host shall fall down, as the leaf falleth off from the vine, and as a falling fig from the fig-tree. For my sword shall be bathed in heaven: behold it shall come down upon Idumea. . . .*" (Isaiah 34:3–5)

Here again we have the very imagery used by our Lord in His prophetic discourse; and if the fate of Bozrah might properly be described in language so lofty, why should it be thought extravagant to employ similar terms in describing the fate of Jerusalem?[23]

At this point we cannot accuse Russell of deviating from the classical Reformed hermeneutic that requires us to interpret Scripture by Scripture. This is a clear application of the *analogy of faith.*

Though Calvin does not apply this imagery to the fall of Jerusalem, he does acknowledge that this language is poetic:

In what manner *the sun will be darkened* we cannot now conjecture, but the event will show. He does not indeed mean that *the stars* will actually fall, but according to the apprehension of men; and accordingly Luke only predicts that *there will be* SIGNS *in the sun, and in the moon, and in the stars.* The meaning therefore is, that there will be such a violent commotion of the firmament of heaven, that *the stars* themselves will be supposed *to fall.* Luke also adds that there will be a dreadful commotion of the sea, *the sea and the waves roaring, so that men will faint through fear* and alarm. In a word, all the creatures above and below will be, as it were, heralds to summon men to that tribunal, which they will continue to treat with ungodly and wanton contempt till the last day.[24]

Russell and Calvin agree that the language employed in biblical prophecy is not always cold and logical as is common in the Western world, but adopts a kind of fervor common to the East. Scripture commonly describes the visitation of God's judgment with images of convulsion and cataclysms. "The conclusion then to which we are irresistibly led," Russell adds, "is, that the imagery employed by our Lord in this prophetic discourse is not inappropriate to the dissolution of the Jewish state and polity which took place at the destruction of Jerusalem. It is appropriate, both as it is in keeping with the acknowledged style of the ancient prophets, and also because the moral grandeur of the event is such as to justify the use of such language in this particular case."[25]

It remains to be seen how Russell deals with the text in Acts, the language of which is not so steeped in such cataclysmic terms. "The expression 'in like manner' must not be pressed too far," writes Russell. "There are obvious points of difference between the manner of the Ascension and the Parousia. He departed alone, and without visible splendour; He was to return in glory with His angels. The words, however, imply that His coming was to be visible and personal, which would exclude the interpretation which regards it as *providential,* or *spiritual.* The visibility of the Parousia is supported by the uniform teaching of the apostles and the belief of the early Christians: 'Every eye shall see him' (Rev. 1:7)."[26]

Russell's treatment of this text is somewhat terse and less than satisfying. Though he does not wish to push the text too far, it seems to me he hardly pushes it at all. He says Jesus departed "without visible splendor." What were the disciples gazing at? That Jesus ascended in a cloud suggests the presence of the Shekina, which is *manifest* glory and splendor. Russell argues that Jesus' return would be with glory and with his angels and that this would be notably different from his ascension. Yet Jesus' ascension was attended by both glory and angels.

Russell acknowledges that in the record of the ascension there is no reference to the *time* of Jesus' return. But he contends that since the announcement of Jesus' return was made to the disciples, they could reasonably assume that he would return to them in this world and that they would see him in a "little while." Russell believes this is why the disciples returned to Jerusalem in great joy despite the fact that Jesus had just been taken from their midst.

The Parable of the Fig Tree

The Olivet Discourse continues with the parable of the fig tree: "Now learn this parable from the fig tree: When its branch has already become tender and puts forth leaves, you know that summer is near. So you also, when you see all these things, know that it is near, at the very doors." (Matt. 24:32–33)

Before uttering the most controversial portion of the discourse, the reference to the present generation that will not pass away, Jesus gives the brief parable of the fig tree. Russell believes this parable functions as a prefatory statement to the reference to "this generation."

> But, as if to preclude even the possibility of misconception or mistake, our Lord in the next paragraph draws around His prophecy a line so plain and palpable, shutting it wholly within a limit so definite and distinct, that it ought to be decisive of the whole question. . . .
> Words have no meaning if this language, uttered on so solemn an occasion, and so precise and express in its import, does not affirm the near approach of the great event which occupies the whole discourse of our Lord. First the parable of the fig-tree intimates that as the buds on the trees betoken the near approach of summer, so the signs which He had just specified would betoken that the predicted consummation was at hand. *They,* the disciples to whom He was speaking, were to see them, and when they saw them to recognise that the end was "*near, even at the doors.*"[27]

Gary DeMar notes that some interpreters of this parable, most notably Dispensationalists, think it points forward to the Jews returning to Palestine and becoming a nation again. He disagrees, pointing out that there is no mention in the entire New Testament of Israel's becoming a nation again. He agrees with Russell that the parable is linked to the following passage, that Jesus would come within a generation to destroy the temple and Jerusalem.[28]

Though we have not yet reached the end of the Olivet Discourse, I will conclude this chapter at this juncture so we may explore more fully in the next chapter the meaning of Jesus' statement that "this generation shall not pass away" (Matt. 24:34). We can summarize the position of Russell and moderate preterism to this point as follows:

1. The Olivet Discourse contains a continuous and homogeneous prophecy regarding the coming destruction of Jerusalem and the temple, and the parousia of Christ.

2. Several signs will portend these events: the appearance of false christs and false prophets, great social disturbances, natural calamities and convulsions, the persecution of the apostles, the apostasy of professed believers, and the publication of the gospel throughout the Roman empire.
3. The great tribulation refers to the siege of Jerusalem.
4. The Olivet Discourse is not about the end of the world but about the end of a definite time period, the "age of the Jews" or the Jewish dispensation.
5. The graphic language used by Jesus to describe the attending events is metaphorical and consistent with the poetry of fervor used by Old Testament prophets.

This generation will by no means pass away till all these things are fulfilled.

(Matt. 24:34)

What "Generation" Will Witness the End?

As I mentioned in the introduction, the skepticism of Bertrand Russell and the "consistent eschatology" of Johannes Weiss and Albert Schweitzer are directly tied to the time-frame reference of the Olivet Discourse. The crisis of "parousia-delay" eschatology has been fostered in large measure by this problem. Perhaps no other problem has spurred the revival of different strands of preterism and realized eschatology more than has this one.

The Olivet Discourse includes the following:

> [34]". . . Assuredly, I say to you, this generation will by no means pass away till all these things are fulfilled. [35]Heaven and earth will pass away, but My words will by no means pass away.
>
> [36]"But of that day and hour no one knows, no, not even the angels of heaven, but My Father only. [37]But as the days of Noah were, so also will the coming of the Son of Man be. [38]For as in the days before the flood, they were eating and drinking, marrying

and giving in marriage, until the day that Noah entered the ark, [39]and did not know until the flood came and took them all away, so also will the coming of the Son of Man be. . . ."

(Matt. 24:34–39)

Before we examine the preterist view of this portion of the Olivet Discourse, we will make a reconnaissance of various interpretations of the time-frame reference regarding "this generation." David Hill comments on verse 34:

> This verse recalls 16:28, and affirms that some of the disciples would live to see the Parousia. This would presuppose a relatively early date for the event, whereas verse 36 defies all attempts to give a precise chronology.
> Was Jesus in error in his prediction of the nearness of the End, if this saying is regarded as authentic? Attempts to explain this difficulty include the arguments: (a) that the reference is not to the End, but to the Fall of Jerusalem. But are not the accompanying words in 35–36 too solemn to refer simply to some specific historical event? (b) that "this generation" indicates "the people of God" which will survive till the end of time. It is probable that we have here an example of that "shortening of historical perspective" which is so frequent in the prophets.[1]

It is interesting that Hill sees verses 35–36 as basically ruling out the idea that this passage refers to Jerusalem's destruction. Because the day and hour are not known does not preclude the application of a time-frame as lengthy as a human generation. Someone, for example, could predict that an event will take place in the next forty years, and then qualify the prediction by saying "I don't know the particular day or hour" within that span of time. Hill's appeal to the phenomenon of historical-perspective foreshortening is likewise problematic when we remember that Jesus was answering a direct question from his disciples regarding the "when" of his prophecy.

The phrase "this generation will by no means pass away" (Matt. 24:34) is repeated in almost identical language in the accounts of Mark and Luke (see appendix 2). First we notice that Jesus made this statement to his disciples who were alive and present with him at the time. They were the primary audience Jesus was addressing. Indeed subsequent generations of Christians are included by way of extension in the audience of all of Jesus' words. But it is dangerous either to exclude from consideration the original audience or to relegate them to a level of secondary importance.

Two Predictions by Jesus	
Matthew 16:28	There are some standing here who shall not taste death till they see the Son of Man coming in His kingdom.
Matthew 24:34	This generation will by no means pass away till all these things are fulfilled.

J. Stuart Russell argues that 99 persons in every 100 would immediately understand Jesus to mean that the events he was predicting would fall within the limits of the lifetime of an existing generation. This means, not that every person present will necessarily be alive at the time of the fulfillment, but that many or even most will be.

Another Prediction by Jesus

This immediately calls attention to another of Jesus' time-frame references in the Gospels: "For the Son of Man will come in the glory of His Father with His angels, and then He will reward each according to his works. Assuredly, I say to you, there are some standing here who shall not taste death till they see the Son of Man coming in His kingdom." (Matt. 16:27–28)

Matthew declares that some who were in Christ's immediate presence as he was speaking ("some standing here") would not "taste death" before they would "see the Son of Man coming in His kingdom." The term *coming* that appears in the Greek text of Matthew 16:28 is not the word *parousia*. Nevertheless, Jesus does speak of a "coming" of the Son of Man. The expression "shall not taste death" clearly refers to dying, so we may render the text to mean that some who were hearing Jesus' words on this occasion would not die before witnessing some kind of coming of Jesus. Matthew speaks of the coming of Christ "in His kingdom." Mark speaks of their seeing the kingdom of God come "with power" (9:1), and Luke simply says that they will see the kingdom of God (9:27).

The question then, with respect to these texts, is this: What will the disciples observe before all of them die? The Synoptic Gospels link this coming of the Son of Man with some manifestation of the kingdom of God. Many commentators see this manifestation in various critical moments of redemptive history, such as Christ's resurrection, his ascension, or Pentecost, all of which provide some outward manifestation of the kingly glory of Christ. Many specify the transfiguration, where the coming glory of Jesus is made manifest temporarily.

William L. Lane remarks: "The transfiguration was a momentary, but real (and witnessed) manifestation of Jesus' sovereign power which pointed beyond itself to the parousia, when he will come with 'power and glory' (Mark 13:26). The fulfillment of Jesus' promise a short time after the transfiguration (Mark 9:2) provided encouragement to the harassed Christians in Rome and elsewhere that their commitment to Jesus and the gospel was valid." Lane cites J. Schierse to confirm the link between the transfiguration and the parousia. The two events are by no means identical, but the former bears witness to the latter.[2]

That events like the transfiguration and resurrection are manifestations of the coming of God's kingdom is hardly in dispute among most New Testament scholars. The only problem with this linkage is the time-frame reference. In this case, however, it is not that the time-frame is too remote or temporally disconnected from the prediction. Rather it is that the time-frame reference is too *near*. In Mark's Gospel the account of the transfiguration is set in the very next verse, and this verse begins with a specific time reference: "After six days . . ." (9:2). If Jesus' prediction to the disciples is fulfilled within one week (or a few weeks, if the prediction refers to the resurrection, ascension, or Pentecost), why would he specify that these events will occur before "some [of them] standing here . . . will . . . taste death" [9:1]? It seems strange that Jesus would say, "Some of you will not die this week."

One could conceivably argue that Jesus did not know this "coming" would occur so rapidly, that he knew only that it would occur before all of his disciples died. He obviously had some idea of the time-span in which his prediction would be fulfilled. That must be the case to warrant his saying that it would occur before all of his disciples died. But if the prediction came to pass in just six days, this would indicate on Jesus' part a radical misconception of the amount of time that would elapse before the prophecy was fulfilled. This does not mean that Lane's and others' interpretation that this prophecy refers to the transfiguration is impossible. It does suggest, however, that it is unlikely. If Jesus had in view the destruction of Jerusalem, it would make more sense for him to locate the time-frame within a period of several years than within a few days or a few weeks. The time-frame indicated by the reference to some surviving death strongly suggests that there would be an interlude of several years between the prophecy and its fulfillment.

The importance of this consideration is its relationship to our understanding of the disputed time-frame reference in the Olivet Discourse (Matt. 24:34) regarding the passing of a generation. If Jesus had in mind a time-frame of roughly forty years, it could also be said that during this time-frame some of his disciples would not taste death. If the Olivet Discourse refers primarily to events surrounding the destruction of Jerusalem and if the word *generation* refers to a forty-year period, then it is possible, if not probable, that Jesus' reference to his coming in Matthew 16:28 refers to the same events, not to the transfiguration or other close-at-hand events.

With respect to Jesus' remarks in Matthew 16, J. Stuart Russell takes a strong position:

> This remarkable declaration is of the greatest importance in this discussion, and may be regarded as the key to the right interpretation of the New Testament doctrine of the Parousia. Though it cannot be said that there are any special difficulties in the language, it has greatly perplexed the commentators, who are much divided in their explanations. It is surely unnecessary to ask what

is the *coming of the Son of man* here predicted. To suppose that it refers merely to the glorious manifestation of Jesus on the mount of transfiguration, though an hypothesis which has great names to support it, is so palpably inadequate as an interpretation that it scarcely requires refutation. . . .

It is enough to say that such an interpretation of our Saviour's words could never have entered into the minds of those who heard them. . . . How could the resurrection of Christ be called—His coming in the glory of His Father, with the holy angels, in His kingdom, and to judgment?[3]

Russell also argues that Jesus' manner of speaking would better suit an interval of thirty or forty years, a time-frame in which it would be reasonable to expect that some of those present would die, but not all. Russell also sees a link to Jesus' statement in Matthew 10: "But when they persecute you in this city, flee to another. For assuredly, I say to you, you will not have gone through the cities of Israel before the Son of Man comes" (Matt. 10:23).

"In this passage" writes Russell, "we find the earliest distinct mention of that great event which we shall find so frequently alluded to henceforth by our Lord and His apostles, viz., His coming again, or the Parousia. . . . Who can doubt that 'the coming of the Son of man' is here, what it is everywhere else, the formula by which the Parousia, the second coming of Christ, is expressed? This phrase has a definite and consistent signification, as much as His crucifixion, or His resurrection, and admits of no other interpretation in this place."[4]

Again, if Russell is correct in concluding that the coming referred to in this text is the parousia of Christ, then the primary time-frame for the parousia must be restricted to a forty-year period. It surely did not take the disciples much more than forty years to cover the boundaries of Palestine with the gospel message.

The Meaning of "This Generation"

The texts we have examined are relevant to the central question we are facing: What is meant by the phrase "this generation will not pass away" in the Olivet Discourse? Russell argues that its *prima facie* meaning can only be a period no longer than the life-span of a generation, which is thirty to forty years. He says:

> Far, however, from accepting this decision of our Lord as final, the commentators have violently resisted that which seems the natural and common-sense meaning of His words. They have insisted that because the events predicted did not so come to pass in that generation, therefore the word *generation (genea)* cannot possibly mean, what it is usually understood to mean, the people of that particular age or period, the contemporaries of our Lord. To affirm that these things did not come to pass is to beg the question, and something more. But we submit that it is the business of grammarians not to be apprehensive of possible consequences, but to settle the true meaning of words. Our Lord's predictions may be safely left to take care of themselves; it is for us to try to understand them.[5]

Gary DeMar takes a similar tack with respect to the meaning of the phrase "this generation": "The futurist interpreters of Matthew 24 assert that 'this generation' does not mean the generation to whom Jesus was speaking. Rather, it refers to a distant generation alive at the time when these events will take place."[6]

I think DeMar commits a basic error at this point. Futurists do not tend to argue that Jesus was not speaking to that generation of his contemporaries. Rather they argue that the term *generation* here refers not to a specific time-frame of forty years, but to a "kind" or "sort" of people. Some of these interpreters see "this generation" as a description of believers, while others see it as a description of the wicked. That is, Jesus may be saying that believers like the disciples will not pass from the earth before Jesus appears in his parousia. This does not exclude the original disciples from being numbered among "this generation." Similarly Jesus could have meant that, no matter how long he tarries before his parousia, there will be present generations of wicked people who will resist the kingdom of Christ.

Herman Ridderbos champions such a view:

A fuller study and closer examination of this passage may, however, favor a different view. The great question is, does Jesus mention a particular *terminal date,* or does he only speak of the *certainty* of the things he has foretold? The supposition that he means a certain terminal date here remains striking in connection with the fact that a moment later he says, "but of that day and of that hour knoweth no man" [Matt. 24:36]. Although we need not speak of a discrepancy (as [W. G.] Kümmel does) because we might explain the text by saying, "but of the date and the exact point of time no man knows"; the force of this pronouncement would be considerably weakened by this restriction of the fulfillment to the contemporary generation. . . . In this case, we must not attribute a temporal meaning to the words "this generation," but must conceive of it in the unfavorable sense in which it occurs also elsewhere, viz., the people of this particular disposition and frame of mind who are averse to Jesus and his words.[7]

Ridderbos sees the phrase "this generation" as referring not to a frame of *time* but to a frame of *mind.* He argues that Jesus' purpose is to underline the *certainty* of his coming and not the time of it.

One of the chief problems with this interpretation is that Jesus was answering not a question of certainty, but a question regarding chronology. The disciples were not asking *if* these things would come to pass. They were asking *when* they would come to pass.

DeMar argues that to interpret "this generation" as meaning something other than the generation to which Jesus was speaking is to interpret the word *generation* in a manner that is alien to its primary meaning in the New Testament. He says:

> . . . the use of "this generation" throughout the Gospels makes it clear that it means the generation to whom Jesus was speaking. It never means "race," as some claim, or some future generation. The adjective *this* points to the contemporary nature of the generation. If some future generation had been in view, Jesus could have chosen the adjective *that:* "That [future] generation which begins with the budding of the fig tree [Israel regathered to the

land of her fathers] will not pass away until all these things take place."

   . . . "Of the thirty-eight appearances of *genea* apart from Luke 21:32//Matthew 24:34//Mark 13:30 all have the temporal meaning, primarily that of 'contemporaries.'" . . .[8]

DeMar then quotes David Chilton: "*Not one* of these references is speaking of the entire Jewish race over thousands of years; *all* use the word in its normal sense of *the sum total of those living at the same time*. It always refers to *contemporaries*. (In fact, those who say it means 'race' tend to acknowledge this fact, but explain that the word suddenly *changes* its meaning when Jesus uses it in Matthew 24!)"[9]

Russell argues in a similar manner:

> It is contended by many that in this place the word *genea* should be rendered '*race*, or *nation*'; and that our Lord's words mean no more than that the Jewish race or nation should not pass away, or perish, until the predictions which He had just uttered had come to pass. . . . It is true, no doubt, that the word *genea*, like most others, has different shades of meaning, and that sometimes, in the Septuagint and in classic authors it may refer to a nation or a race. But we think that it is demonstrable without any shadow of doubt that the expression '*this generation*,' so often employed by our Lord, always refers solely and exclusively to *His contemporaries, the Jewish people of His own period*. It might safely be left to the candid judgment of every reader, whether a Greek scholar or not, whether this is not so: but as the point is one of great importance, it may be desirable to adduce the proofs of this assertion.[10]

Before we look at these proofs, it is important to note Russell's surprising claim that the universal meaning of "this generation" for Christ can be demonstrated beyond the shadow of doubt. This is startling because alternate renderings of the phrase have been offered by some of the most respected scholars. Of course Russell is not saying that no doubt exists on the matter. Rather he is claiming that his view is *demonstrable without shadow of doubt*. What is in dispute among scholars should not be in dispute, Russell contends, and he promises to prove his point conclusively.

Russell makes a crucial admission, one that makes it all the more difficult to prove his point. He admits that *genea* is capable of variant shades of meaning and that there are instances in the Septuagint and classical sources where the term means something other than a contemporary group of people who live within a definite time-frame. To prove his point he must show that every time Jesus uses the term, it refers, solely and exclusively, to his contemporaries.

Russell's Case

Let us look at the argument Russell provides to make his case:

1. In our Lord's final address to the people, delivered on the same day as this discourse on the Mount of Olives, He declared, "All these things shall come upon *this generation*" (Matt. 23:36). No commentator has ever proposed to understand this as referring to any other than the *existing* generation.
2. "Whereunto shall I liken this generation?" (Matt. 11:16) Here it is admitted by [John Peter] Lange and [Rudolf] Stier that the word refers to "*the then existing last generation of Israel.*"
3. "An evil and adulterous *generation* seeketh after a sign." "The men of Nineveh shall rise up in the judgment with *this generation.*" "The Queen of the South shall rise up in the judgment with *this generation.*" "Even so shall it be also unto *this* wicked *generation*" (Matt. 12:39, 41, 42, 45). . . . Surely the generation which sought after a sign was the *then existing generation*; and can it be supposed that it was against any other generation than that which had resisted such preaching as that of John the Baptist and of Christ that the Gentiles were to rise up in the judgment? There is only one interpretation of our Lord's language possible, and it is that which refers His words to His own perverse and unbelieving contemporaries.

4. "That the blood of all the prophets . . . may be required of *this generation.*" "It shall be required of *this generation.*" (Luke 11:50, 51)
5. "Whoever shall be ashamed of me in *this* adulterous and sinful *generation*" (Mark 8:38).
6. "The Son of man must be rejected of *this generation*" (Luke 17:25). . . .

These are all the examples in which the expression '*this generation*' occurs in the sayings of our Lord, and they establish beyond all reasonable question the reference of the words in the important declaration now before us. . . .[11]

We note a subtle shift from "demonstrable without any shadow of doubt" to "beyond all reasonable question." Perhaps the shift is merely stylistic, but technically there is a difference between proving something beyond a shadow of doubt and proving it beyond a reasonable doubt. We understand this difference keenly in our modern judicial system, where the jury in a criminal trial is called to reach a verdict beyond a reasonable doubt, which clearly is less than beyond a shadow of doubt.

It is one thing to say that Russell's evidence is "reasonable," it is quite another to declare that it is rationally compelling. This is especially significant in that Russell has so far offered a mere restatement of texts in which Jesus refers to *this generation,* providing little commentary. Russell seems to assume that the meaning of Jesus' words in these texts is self-evident.

Russell seeks to buttress his case by using the classic *reductio ad absurdum* form of argument:

But suppose that we were to adopt the rendering proposed, and take *genea* as meaning a *race,* what point or significance would there be in the prediction then? Can any one believe that the assertion so solemnly made by our Lord, "Verily I say unto you," etc., amounts to no more than this, "The Hebrew race shall not become extinct till all these things be fulfilled"? Imagine a prophet in our own times predicting a great catastrophe in which London would be destroyed, St. Paul's and the Houses of Parliament levelled with the ground, and a fearful slaughter of the inhabitants be perpetrated; and that when asked, "When shall these things come to pass?" he should reply, "The Anglo-Saxon race shall not become extinct till all these things be fulfilled"! Would this be a satisfactory answer? Would not such an answer be considered derogatory to the prophet, and an affront to his hearers? Would they not have reason to say, "It is safe prophesying when the event is placed at an interminable distance!" But the bare supposition of such a sense in our Lord's prediction shows itself to be a *reductio ad absurdum.* Was it for this that the disciples were to wait and watch? . . . Such a hypothesis is its own refutation.[12]

Russell's argument applies to the interpretation of *generation* as "a race." He acknowledges other interpretations of *genea,* such as a generation of righteous people or of wicked people, but he believes these alternatives require no consideration. He then proceeds to consider how long a generation is usually thought to be, concluding that, though it is indefinite, it falls within the limits of approximately thirty or forty years. He cites Old Testament references supporting this view. He places the destruction of Jerusalem within the time-frame of 37 years after the Olivet Discourse.

I do not agree that Russell proves his point beyond a shadow of doubt. I do think, however, that he gives weighty evidence that with the phrase "this generation" Jesus refers to his contemporaries and that Jesus points to a definite period of time within which this generation would die.

Additional Evidence

The entry on *genea* in Gerhard Kittel's *Theological Dictionary of the New Testament* says that in general usage *genea* means "birth" or "descent," but that it can also mean "generation." The Septuagint uses it chiefly to mean "'generation' in the sense of contemporaries." In the New Testament, "as a purely formal concept *[genea]* is always qualified," the entry declares. "It mostly denotes 'generation' in the sense of contemporaries."[13] The phrase *this generation* "is to be understood temporally, but there is always a qualifying criticism" (such as "adulterous," "evil," "unbelieving").[14]

William L. Lane agrees that the phrase "this generation" refers to the contemporaries of Jesus. "The significance of the temporal reference has been debated," Lane writes in his commentary on Mark, "but in Mark 'this generation' clearly designates the contemporaries of Jesus . . . and there is no consideration from the context which lends support to any other proposal. Jesus solemnly affirms that the generation contemporary with his disciples will witness the fulfillment of his prophetic word, culminating in the destruction of Jerusalem and the dismantling of the Temple. With this word Jesus responds to the initial question of the disciples regarding the time when 'these things' will take place."[15]

There seems to be widespread agreement that "this generation" refers to the contemporaries of Jesus and not to some future group. This view is held not only by preterists such as J. Stuart Russell, but by critics such as Bertrand Russell, the consistent eschatology school, and contemporary conservative scholars such as Lane. With this much support, one wonders why the Olivet Discourse is not seen as having been fulfilled in the first century.

We remember that for J. Stuart Russell's case to hold, it is necessary to conclude not only that "this generation" refers to Jesus' contemporaries, but also that "all these things" includes Jesus' parousia. To avoid Russell's conclusion, some have argued that "this generation" means something other than Jesus' contemporaries or that "all these things" refers exclusively to the events surrounding the destruction of Jerusalem.

Herman Ridderbos provides an interesting summary of this:

The phrase "all (these) things," however, is then given a limiting interpretation. Thus [Seakle] Greijdanus, e.g., writes that this "all" is of course not unlimited; it is not all that must happen to the world according to the divine counsel, it is not the whole of the history of the world, but that which our Lord announces with respect to the generation that he mentions here, that which is especially concerned with that generation, so in particular that which he has indicated and foretold in [Matthew 24] verses 20–24, namely, all the distress that was to come to the Jewish people of that time and that would destroy and annihilate them. In view of this opinion, this "of course" in Greijdanus apparently means, "because this pronouncement would otherwise not have been realized." So this is an *explicatio ex eventu*.[16]

Ridderbos gets to the crux of the matter. Attempts to interpret "this generation" as referring to something other than Jesus' contemporaries exclusively, or to restrict "all these things" to the events surrounding Jerusalem's destruction are driven by a desire to preserve the biblical text and the words of Christ from being proven false. The issue of parousia-delay in consistent eschatology lurks not far below the surface. Though Ridderbos does not accept the preterist view, favoring the "already and not yet" hypothesis, he nevertheless argues against restricting the phrase "all these things" to the destruction of Jerusalem. He says:

> There may be some doubt as to whether the phrase "all (these) things" denotes the whole of the signs, as well as the *parousia* of the Son of Man. The expression in the 33rd verse of Matthew 24, "when ye shall see all these things, *know that it is near, even at the doors,*" would seem to favor the view that "all these things" refers to the signs. On the other hand, that which follows after Matthew 24:34, as well as that after the parallel text in Mark 13:30, clearly refers to the *parousia* also, "But of that day and of that hour knoweth no man," etc. Therefore, in our opinion, the rigorous restriction of the words "all (these) things" to the signs alone, with the exclusion of the *parousia* proper, is not justified. . . . But to our mind, it is perfectly arbitrary to refuse to take these signs into account in verses 31 and 32. The text explicitly says *"these things"* and *"all,"* both clearly referring to all that has gone before. Consequently, whatever difficulties these passages may offer, it is not permissible, we think, to get rid of them by making arbitrary restrictions in the meaning of the text.[17]

If both "this generation" and "all these things" are taken at face value, then either all the content of Jesus' Olivet Discourse, including the parousia he describes here, have already taken place (in some sense), or at least some of Jesus' prophecy failed to take place within the time-frame assigned to it. Evangelical scholars have opted for some form of the former option, critical scholars for the latter.

Questions for Preterists

If it is agreed that "all these things" described in the discourse took place in the first century, then some crucial questions remain: (1) How can it be said that they in fact did take place? And (2) if they did take place, what about the Christian's hope for a future return of Jesus? These two questions exercise enormous influence on the theories presented in response.

How one approaches the contents of the Olivet Discourse depends largely on the hermeneutic (the principles of interpretation) employed. The orthodox Protestant hermeneutic follows Martin Luther's view of the *sensus literalis*. There is much confusion today regarding the "literal sense" of Scripture. Luther means that one should interpret the Bible according to the manner in which it was written, or in its "literary sense." This was an attempt to prevent fanciful flights into subjectivism by which the Scriptures are turned into a "wax nose," twisted and shaped according to the interpreter's whim or bias. To guard against subjectivism, Luther sought a rule that would guide the interpreter to an objective rendering of the text.

To interpret the Bible "literally" in the classical sense requires that we learn to recognize in Scripture different genres of literature. Poetry is to be interpreted as poetry, and didactic passages are to be interpreted according to the grammar of the didactic. Historical narrative must not be treated as parable, nor parable as strict historical narrative. Much of biblical prophecy is cast in an apocalyptic genre that employs graphic imaginative language and often mixes elements of common historical narrative with the figurative language of poetry.

Part of the confusion concerning biblical interpretation stems from contemporary usage of the term *literal*. *Literal* today usually refers, not to the technical sense in which Luther used it, but to the interpretation of poetic images and the like as straightforward didactic or indicative language. To take every text "literally" in this sense is not to interpret it according to the genre in which it is written, but to interpret it in a plain indicative sense. When the Olivet Discourse is subjected to such a wooden literalism, the crisis of parousia-delay is created. The cataclysmic events surrounding the parousia as predicted in the Olivet Discourse obviously did not occur "literally" in A.D. 70. Some elements of the discourse did take place "literally," but others obviously did not.

This problem of literal fulfillment leaves us with three basic solutions to interpreting the Olivet Discourse:

1. We can interpret the entire discourse literally. In this case we must conclude that some elements of Jesus' prophecy failed to come to pass, as advocates of "consistent eschatology" maintain.
2. We can interpret the events surrounding the predicted parousia literally and interpret the time-frame references figuratively. This method is employed chiefly by those who do not restrict the phrase "this generation will not pass away . . ." to the life span of Jesus' contemporaries.
3. We can interpret the time-frame references literally and the events surrounding the parousia figuratively. In this view, all of Jesus' prophecies in the Olivet Discourse were fulfilled during the period between the discourse itself and the destruction of Jerusalem in A.D. 70.

The third option is followed by preterists. The strength of the preterist position is found precisely in this hermeneutical method. When faced with the option of interpreting the time-frame references literally or interpreting the description of the parousia literally, the preterist chooses the former. The preterist's choice is governed by a larger hermeneutical principle, namely the principle of interpreting Scripture by Scripture *(analogia fide)*. As Russell has shown, there is much biblical precedent for interpreting figuratively references to astronomical upheavals in biblical prophecies of catastrophic events. On the other hand, the time-frame references are not clothed in such imagery, but are expressed in straightforward, ordinary language. Following Luther's view of seeking the "plain sense" of a Scripture passage, preterists insist on interpreting the time-frame references in their *prima facie* ("plain") sense.

The three options mentioned above do not totally exhaust the possibilities. Other alternatives have been given. As we will see later, some preterists argue for a "literal" fulfillment of the entire discourse within the time span of a single human generation.

Another method is to apply the principle of primary and secondary fulfillment of biblical prophecies (a method Russell strongly eschews). Advocates of this method see an early *primary* fulfillment of prophecy (a partial fulfillment), followed at a later time by a *secondary* fulfillment (the complete or ultimate fulfillment). This method has been applied, for example, to Isaiah's prophecies concerning the virgin birth and the Suffering Servant of God.

Russell reacts strongly against such attempts to interpret the Olivet Discourse:

> The commonly received view of the structure of this discourse, which is almost taken for granted, alike by expositors and by the generality of readers, is, that our Lord, in answering the question of His disciples respecting the destruction of the temple, mixes up with that event the destruction of the world, the universal judgment, and the final consummation of all things. . . .
>
> An objection may be taken, *in limine,* to the principles involved in this method of interpreting Scripture. Are we to look for double, triple, and multiple meanings, for prophecies within prophecies, and mysteries wrapped in mysteries, where we might reasonably have expected a plain answer to a plain question? Can any one be sure of understanding the Scriptures if they are thus enigmatic and obscure?[18]

The simple reply to Russell's questions, posed in rhetorical fashion, is that at times the Scriptures are enigmatic and obscure. Luther and the magisterial Reformers did teach the perspicuity of Scripture, maintaining that the Scriptures *as a whole* are clear. They did not deny, however, that certain passages are indeed enigmatic. Hence the rule that calls for interpreting the obscure in light of the clear, rather than the clear in light of the obscure.

The second problem posed by preterism, and by far the most crucial, is whether there remains a future hope for the church. Is the "blessed hope" for a future, consummate parousia of Christ, an article of faith for historic Christianity, a false hope? Is the eschatology that includes the parousia to be reduced to an utterly "realized eschatology"?

These questions require that we distinguish between *moderate preterism* and *radical preterism*. Moderate preterism, though it sees the coming of Christ predicted in the Olivet Discourse as having been already fulfilled, still believes in a future consummation of Christ and his kingdom, based on other New Testament texts (which we will explore later). Radical preterism, on the other hand, sees virtually the entire New Testament eschatology as having been realized already.

*Jerusalem will be trampled
by Gentiles
until the times of the Gentiles
are fulfilled.*

(Luke 21:24)

3

What "Age" Was about to End?

C losely linked to the issues surrounding the time-frame question of the Olivet Discourse is the question of the biblical meaning of "the end of the age." Does this phrase point to the end of world history, the final consummation of the kingdom of Christ? Or does it refer to the end of a particular divine economy, namely the one in which Old Testament Israel figures prominently? In other words, does the phrase "the end of the age" refer to the end of the *Jewish* age?

Fundamental to preterism is the contention that the phrase "the end of the age" refers specifically to the end of the Jewish age and the beginning of the age of the Gentiles, or the church age. J. Stuart Russell begins his exposition of this concept by referring to the content of Matthew 13:

> Then Jesus sent the multitude away and went into the house. And His disciples came to Him, saying, "Explain to us the parable of the tares of the field." He answered and said to them: "He who

sows the good seed is the Son of Man. The field is the world, the good seeds are the sons of the kingdom, but the tares are the sons of the wicked *one*. The enemy who sowed them is the devil, the harvest is the end of the age, and the reapers are the angels. Therefore as the tares are gathered and burned in the fire, so it will be at the end of this age. The Son of Man will send out His angels, and they will gather out of His kingdom all things that offend, and those who practice lawlessness, and will cast them into the furnace of fire. There will be wailing and gnashing of teeth. Then the righteous will shine forth as the sun in the kingdom of their Father. He who has ears to hear, let him hear!

"Again, the kingdom of heaven is like treasure hidden in a field, which a man found and hid; and for joy over it he goes and sells all that he has and buys that field.

"Again, the kingdom of heaven is like a merchant seeking beautiful pearls, who, when he had found one pearl of great price, went and sold all that he had and bought it.

"Again, the kingdom of heaven is like a dragnet that was cast into the sea and gathered some of every kind, which, when it was full, they drew to shore; and they sat down and gathered the good into vessels, but threw the bad away. So it will be at the end of the age. The angels will come forth, separate the wicked from among the just, and cast them into the furnace of fire. There will be wailing and gnashing of teeth."

(Matt. 13:36–50)

Verses 38–40 are translated as follows in the King James Version:

[38]The field is the world; the good seed are the children of the kingdom; but the tares are the children of the wicked one; [39]the enemy that sowed them is the devil; the harvest is the end of the world; and the reapers are the angels. [40]As therefore the tares are gathered and burned in the fire; so shall it be in the end of this world.

Russell comments:

We find in the passages here quoted an example of one of those erroneous renderings which have done much to confuse and mis-

Table 3.1

The World in Matthew 13:38–40

Verse	KJV	NKJV	Greek
38	The field is **the world,** the good seed are the children of the kingdom; but the tares are the children of the wicked one;	The field is **the world,** the good seeds are the sons of the kingdom, but the tares are the sons of the wicked one.	*kosmos*
39	the enemy that sowed them is the devil; the harvest is the end of **the world;** and the reapers are the angels.	The enemy who sowed them is the devil, the harvest is the end of **the age,** and the reapers are the angels.	*aiōn*
40	As therefore the tares are gathered and burned in the fire; so shall it be in the end of **this world.**	Therefore as the tares are gathered and burned in the fire, so it will be at the end of **this age.**	*aiōn*

lead the ordinary readers of our English version [the KJV]. It is probable, that ninety-nine in every hundred understand by the phrase, "the end of the world" the close of human history, and the destruction of the material earth. They would not imagine that the "world" in ver. 38 and the "world" in ver. 39, 40, are totally different words, with totally different meanings. Yet such is the fact. *Kosmos* in ver. 38 is rightly translated *world,* and refers to the world of men, but *aiōn* in ver. 39, 40, refers to a *period of time,* and should be rendered *age* or *epoch.* . . . It is of the greatest importance to understand correctly the true meaning of this word, and of the phrase *"the end of the aeon, or age."* *Aiōn* is, as we have said, a period of time, or an age. It is exactly equivalent to the Latin word *aevum,* which is merely *aiōn* in a Latin dress; and the phrase, *sun-*

phrase, *sunteleia tou aiom nos,* translated in our English version, "the end of the world," should be, "the close of the age."[1]

Russell argues that the end of the age signals not merely an "end," but a consummation of one age that is followed immediately by another. This was part of the traditional view of the Jews with regard to their Messiah. The new age that would be inaugurated by the appearance of the Messiah would be called the "kingdom of heaven." The existing age was the Jewish dispensation, which was drawing to a close. This idea was central to the preaching of John the Baptist, who spoke of the time that was "at hand."

The New Testament views the incarnation of Jesus as a time of *crisis.* The English word *crisis* comes from (and is a transliteration of) the Greek word *krisis,* the New Testament word for "judgment." The coming of the Messiah is directly linked to the impending judgment of Israel. John called the nation to repentance and to cleansing by baptism because the Jews were not ready for this crisis, the "visitation" of God in the person of the heavenly Judge, the Son of Man. This visitation was a two-edged sword, a time of redemption for those who welcomed his coming and a time of judgment for those who rejected him.

Under the influence of the Holy Spirit, Zacharias prophesied: "Blessed is the Lord God of Israel, for He has visited and redeemed His people" (Luke 1:68). The word translated "visited" comes from the Greek verb whose corresponding noun is the word *episcopus.* This term comes into the English language as *episcopal,* which refers to a type of church government wherein authority is located in bishops. The term *episcopus* itself is most often translated "bishop." In a literal sense the visitation of God is a divine act of bishoping. In ancient Greek culture a bishop was not a religious figure but a military one. He reviewed the troops to gauge their preparedness for battle. If the bishop found the troops unprepared for battle, sharp penalties would befall them.

The word *episcopus* derived from the root term *scopus,* from which we get the word *scope.* A scope is an instrument used for looking at something. For example we have *microscopes, tele-*

are small *(micro);* a telescope, things that are far away; and a periscope, things that are "around" *(peri).* The prefix *epi-*, when added to a root-word, serves to intensify its meaning. Thus the term *episcopus* refers to someone who looks intently, closely scrutinizing and evaluating an object. The term *bishop* describes a "supervisor," one who gives "super-vision."

When God "visits" his people in the New Testament sense, he comes to examine their condition. He comes to praise or to judge, to redeem or to damn. His coming involves a final examination.

The Day of the Lord

The idea of God visiting his people is closely linked in the Old Testament to the coming "day of the Lord." The phrase "day of the Lord" figures heavily in Old Testament prophecy. Originally it was a day of redemption that the people anticipated with great joy. As the faith and practice of the nation of Israel degenerates, the phrase undergoes a development. It becomes loaded more and more with forecasts of doom and judgment. Yet it also retains a note of hope for the faithful.

The very last prophecy in the Old Testament is found in the book of the prophet Malachi:

> "For behold, the day is coming, burning like an oven, and all the proud, yes, all who do wickedly will be stubble. And the day which is coming shall burn them up," says the LORD of hosts, "that will leave them neither root nor branch. But to you who fear My name the Sun of Righteousness shall arise with healing in His wings; and you shall go out and grow fat like stall-fed calves. You shall trample the wicked, for they shall be ashes under the soles of your feet on the day that I do this," says the LORD of hosts. "Remember the Law of Moses, My servant, which I commanded him in Horeb for all Israel, with the statutes and judgments. Behold, I will send you Elijah the prophet before the coming of the great and dreadful day of the LORD."
>
> *(Mal. 4:1–5)*

The coming day is a "burning oven" that will consume the wicked, yet this day will also herald the Sun of Righteousness, who will come with healing in his wings. Elijah will appear before this "great and dreadful" day. The day of the Lord will be a great day for Israel, but it will also be a dreadful day. This is the crisis of the coming of the Son of Man.

Hobart E. Freeman writes about the day of the Lord in the writing of the prophet Joel: "The central theme of the book is the emphasis upon the *day of the Lord*. This unique eschatological phrase 'the day of Yahweh,' which was first noted in Obadiah (v. 15), is reiterated again and again by the Prophet Joel (1:15; 2: 1–2, 11, 31; 3:14, 18). Its spiritual significance is to be found in the nature and purpose of this day; it is to be a day of wrath and judgment upon the wicked and a day of salvation to the righteous."[2]

Freeman sees a link between Joel's prophecy of the day of the Lord and Christ's predictions in the Olivet Discourse. Freeman believes it refers to an event that is yet to occur in the future: "The day of Yahweh will be heralded by divine portents: 'And I will show wonders in the heavens and in the earth: blood, and fire, and pillars of smoke. The sun shall be turned into darkness, and the moon into blood, before the great and terrible day of Yahweh cometh' (Joel 2:30–31). Quite evidently such apocalyptic phenomena did not find fulfillment at Pentecost, but point to the latter days and the second advent, as our Lord Himself confirms in Matthew 24:29–30, where He uses the same apocalyptic imagery in connection with His second coming."[3]

Freeman sees the link between the day of the Lord and the catastrophic signs enumerated in the Olivet Discourse. He argues that it is "quite evident" that these things were not fulfilled at Pentecost. Surely Russell and preterists would agree that Pentecost did not mark the consummation of the day of the Lord. But they would not agree that this day will be delayed until the end of the world. They see the fulfillment occurring much closer to Pentecost, namely in the destruction of Jerusalem.

It is both fascinating and relevant to the present discussion that Peter, as reported in the Book of Acts, sees a fulfillment (at least in part) of Joel's prophecy on the day of Pentecost:

"But this is what was spoken by the prophet Joel: 'And it shall come to pass in the last days, says God, that I will pour out of My Spirit on all flesh; your sons and your daughters shall prophesy, your young men shall see visions, your old men shall dream dreams. And on My menservants and on My maidservants I will pour out My Spirit in those days; and they shall prophesy. I will show wonders in heaven above and signs in the earth beneath: blood and fire and vapor of smoke. The sun shall be turned into darkness, and the moon into blood, before the coming of the great and notable day of the LORD. And it shall come to pass that whoever calls on the name of the LORD shall be saved.'"

(Acts 2:16–21)

In this discourse at Pentecost, Peter says the phenomenon people have just witnessed is the one spoken of by the Prophet Joel. Joel's prophecy is one about the last days and about the signs that would signal the coming day of the Lord. If Freeman is correct in his assessment, then part of Joel's prophecy was fulfilled at Pentecost, but the larger portion of it has remained unfulfilled for thousands of years since then.

Before seeing how Russell handles the prophecies of Joel and Malachi, we shall look at other Old Testament prophecies regarding the day of the Lord. The first is Amos's famous summary of the day of the Lord: "Woe to you who desire the day of the LORD! For what good is the day of the LORD to you? It will be darkness, and not light. It will be as though a man fled from a lion, and a bear met him; or as though he went into the house, leaned his hand on the wall, and a serpent bit him. Is not the day of the LORD darkness, and not light? Is it not very dark, with no brightness in it?" (Amos 5:18–20)

Amos uses the Hebrew literary device of the oracle. This is an oracle of doom, prefaced by the word *woe*. Graphic images describe the irony that will befall those who have a false expectation. They will be like the man who flees from a lion only to be confronted by a bear. Bruce Vawter comments on this text:

The "day of Yahweh" is another of those beliefs older than the prophets, to which Amos refers, as to the "remnant," as needing no explanation. It was to be the day of Yahweh's intervention, his settling of accounts. Faithful Israelites could only yearn for such a day, when the people of God would be vindicated along with Yahweh himself. But the Israel to which Amos was speaking was no longer the people of God. If Yahweh is to take vengeance on his enemies, what will he not do to that people that had become his greatest enemy, that had rejected him not unknowingly but in the full light of knowledge? In keeping with his minimal view of the remnant, Amos' expectation of the day of Yahweh is entirely pessimistic.[4]

Amos's pessimism concerning the day of the Lord is tempered by elements of hope in the prophecies of Hosea, Isaiah, and Zephaniah. Zephaniah says:

> . . . Be silent in the presence of the Lord GOD; for the day of the LORD is at hand, for the LORD has prepared a sacrifice; He has invited His guests. "And it shall be, in the day of the LORD's sacrifice, that I will punish the princes and the king's children, and all such as are clothed with foreign apparel. In the same day I will punish all those who leap over the threshold, who fill their masters' houses with violence and deceit. And there shall be on that day," says the LORD, "the sound of a mournful cry from the Fish Gate, a wailing from the Second Quarter, and a loud crashing from the hills. Wail, you inhabitants of Maktesh! For all the merchant people are cut down; all those who handle money are cut off. And it shall come to pass at that time that I will search Jerusalem with lamps, and punish the men who are settled in complacency, who say in their heart, 'The LORD will not do good, nor will He do evil.' Therefore their goods shall become booty, and their houses a desolation; they shall build houses, but not inhabit them; they shall plant vineyards, but not drink their wine."
> The great day of the LORD is near; it is near and hastens quickly. The noise of the day of the LORD is bitter; there the mighty men shall cry out. That day is a day of wrath, a day of trouble and distress, a day of devastation and desolation, a day of darkness and gloominess, a day of clouds and thick darkness, a day of trumpet and alarm against the fortified cities and against the high towers. "I will bring distress upon men, and they shall walk like blind men,

because they have sinned against the LORD; their blood shall be poured out like dust, and their flesh like refuse."

(Zeph. 1:7–17)

This grim portend of the day of the Lord echoes that of Amos. But later Zephaniah adds to it a note of optimism: "Gather yourselves together, yes, gather together, O undesirable nation, before the decree is issued, before the day passes like chaff, before the LORD's fierce anger comes upon you, before the day of the LORD's anger comes upon you! Seek the LORD, all you meek of the earth, who have upheld His justice. Seek righteousness, seek humility. It may be that you will be hidden in the day of the LORD's anger." (Zeph. 2:1–3)

Russell on the Day of the Lord

In Russell's view the Old Testament prophecies regarding the coming day of the Lord point to the destruction of Jerusalem in A.D. 70. He writes:

That this is no vague and unmeaning threat is evident from the distinct and definite terms in which it is announced. Everything points to an approaching crisis in the history of the nation, when God would inflict judgment upon His rebellious people. "The day" was coming— "the day that shall burn as a furnace"; "the great and terrible day of the Lord." That this "day" refers to a certain period, and a specific event, does not admit of question. . . . and we shall meet with a distinct reference to it in the address of the Apostle Peter on the Day of Pentecost (Acts 2:20). But the period is further more precisely defined by the remarkable statement of Malachi . . . "Behold, I will send you Elijah the prophet before the coming of the great and terrible day of the Lord" [Mal. 4:5]. The explicit declaration of our Lord that the predicted Elijah was no other than His own forerunner, John the Baptist (Matt. 11:14) enables us to determine the time and the event referred to as "the great and terrible day of the Lord." It must be sought at no great distance from the period of John the Baptist. That is to say, the allusion is to the judgment of the Jewish nation, when their city and temple were destroyed, and the entire fabric of the Mosaic polity was dissolved.[5]

Russell argues that these prophecies refer not to Christ's first coming, but to Christ's second coming—in judgment on Jerusalem. At this point we must ask how the day of the Lord relates to the concept of divine visitation *(episcopus)*. We have already noted that at the birth of John the Baptist, Zacharias said that "the Lord has visited and redeemed his people" (Luke 1:68). It would seem then that the day of visitation at least *begins* within the context of the incarnation of Christ, whose herald was John the Baptist. Luke uses the language of visitation with respect to Jesus' earthly ministry.

> Now it happened, the day after, that He went into a city called Nain; and many of His disciples went with Him, and a large crowd. And when He came near the gate of the city, behold, a dead man was being carried out, the only son of his mother; and she was a widow. And a large crowd from the city was with her. When the Lord saw her, He had compassion on her and said to her, "Do not weep." Then He came and touched the open coffin, and those who carried him stood still. And He said, "Young man, I say to you, arise." And he who was dead sat up and began to speak. And He presented him to his mother. Then fear came upon all, and they glorified God, saying, "A great prophet has risen up among us"; and, "God has visited His people." And this report about Him went throughout all Judea and all the surrounding region.
>
> *(Luke 7:11–17)*

Clearly the ministry of Jesus was seen in terms of a divine visitation. Jesus himself used these terms in his lament over Jerusalem on Palm Sunday:

> . . . And some of the Pharisees called to Him from the crowd, "Teacher, rebuke Your disciples." But He answered and said to them, "I tell you that if these should keep silent, the stones would immediately cry out."
> Now as He drew near, He saw the city and wept over it, saying, "If you had known, even you, especially in this your day, the things

that make for your peace! But now they are hidden from your eyes. For the days will come upon you when your enemies will build an embankment around you, surround you and close you in on every side, and level you, and your children within you, to the ground; and they will not leave in you one stone upon another, because you did not know the time of your visitation."

(Luke 19:39–44)

In this lament Jesus speaks of "this your day" in which certain things were unknown to them and concealed from their eyes. Then he speaks of the coming days in which not one stone will be left on another because they were ignorant of the time of their visitation. I. Howard Marshall comments:

> As Jesus sees Jerusalem spread out before him, he weeps over the destruction which will come over it unawares. The city could have learned the way of peace from his teaching, but it would fail to recognise in his coming the gracious presence of God offering a last opportunity of repentance; the attitude of the Pharisees (Luke 19:39–40) would prevail. There would be a different kind of visitation in due course, a judgment in which enemies would destroy the city stone by stone. . . .
> . . . there is no reason to doubt that the Christian interpretation of the fall of Jerusalem as the outcome of failure to accept the message of Jesus goes back to Jesus himself. . . .
> . . . Here the visitation is intended to be the occasion of salvation as proclaimed by Jesus; unrecognised as such, the same visitation becomes the basis for a judgment yet to follow.[6]

We conclude that the day of visitation refers partly to the incarnation. This event brought a double-edged crisis. Jesus' earthly ministry brought the gracious presence of God's redemption to those who received him, but set the stage for a soon-to-occur visitation of wrath and judgment to Jerusalem and the impenitent children of Israel. Here is an "already and not yet," but one that spans about forty years, not centuries or millennia.

Parables about Judgment

Russell sees, then, the day of the Lord's visitation of wrath and judgment on Jerusalem as the time when the Lord comes suddenly to his temple, predicted in Malachi 3:1. He finds Jesus' forecasts of this coming judgment, not only in the Olivet Discourse, but also in other places, particularly in the rash of parables Jesus utters near the end of his public ministry.

With reference to the parable of the pounds (Luke 19:11–27), Russell writes: "It cannot fail to strike every attentive reader of the Gospel history, how much the teaching of our Lord, as He approached the close of His ministry, dwelt upon the theme of coming judgment. When He spoke this parable, He was on His way to Jerusalem to keep His last Passover before He suffered; and it is remarkable how His discourses from this time seem almost wholly engrossed, not by His own approaching death, but the impending catastrophe of the nation."[7]

Russell points beyond the parable of the pounds to Jesus' cursing of the fig tree, parable of the wicked husbandmen, parable of the marriage of the king's son (Matt. 22:1–14), second lamentation over Jerusalem, and woes pronounced on "that generation" (Matt. 23:13–30). Russell sees all of these as references to the catastrophe that is about to befall the Jewish nation. With respect to the parable of the pounds, Russell quotes Augustus Neander favorably:

> In this parable, in view of the circumstances under which it was uttered, and of the approaching catastrophe, special intimations are given of Christ's departure from the earth, of his ascension, and return to judge the rebellious Theocratic nation and consummate his dominion. It describes a great man, who travels to the distant court of the mighty emperor, to receive from him authority over his countrymen, and to return with royal power. So Christ was not immediately recognized in his kingly office, but first had to depart from the earth and leave his agents to advance his kingdom, to ascend into heaven and be appointed Theocratic King, and return again to exercise his contested power.[8]

To understand the full import of what is being claimed here, we need to look at the complete text of the parable:

> Now as they heard these things, He spoke another parable, because He was near Jerusalem and because they thought the kingdom of God would appear immediately. Therefore He said:
> "A certain nobleman went into a far country to receive for himself a kingdom and to return. So he called ten of his servants, delivered to them ten minas, and said to them, 'Do business till I come.' But his citizens hated him, and sent a delegation after him, saying, 'We will not have this man to reign over us.'
> "And so it was that when he returned, having received the kingdom, he then commanded these servants, to whom he had given the money, to be called to him, that he might know how much every man had gained by trading.
> "Then came the first, saying, 'Master, your mina has earned ten minas.'
> "And he said to him, 'Well done, good servant; because you were faithful in a very little, have authority over ten cities.'
> "And the second came, saying, 'Master, your mina has earned five minas.'
> "Likewise he said to him, 'You also be over five cities.'
> "And another came, saying, 'Master, here is your mina, which I have kept put away in a handkerchief. For I feared you, because you are an austere man. You collect what you did not deposit, and reap what you did not sow.'
> "And he said to him, 'Out of your own mouth I will judge you, you wicked servant. You knew that I was an austere man, collecting what I did not deposit and reaping what I did not sow. Why then did you not put my money in the bank, that at my coming I might have collected it with interest?'
> "And he said to those who stood by, 'Take the mina from him, and give it to him who has ten minas.'
> ("But they said to him, 'Master, he has ten minas.')
> "'For I say to you, that to everyone who has will be given; and from him who does not have, even what he has will be taken away from him. But bring here those enemies of mine, who did not want me to reign over them, and slay them before me.'"

(Luke 19:11–26)

According to Russell, Jesus gave this parable to insure that his disciples would not hope that the kingdom was to come *immediately*. He declared that an interval of time must intervene before their expectations were fulfilled. The kingdom was still "at hand," but not as near as the disciples supposed. Christ had to depart, or "go away," for a little while. Russell does not see as an option the idea that Christ would depart for a long while. Christ's departure for a short period was the hope and faith of the early church, and it was not a delusion.

Russell's thesis at this point depends heavily on the assumption that the phrase "the end of the age" refers not to the end of history or the end of the world, but to the end of the *Jewish* age. There are four references in Matthew's Gospel to "the end of the age." None explicitly specifies the *Jewish* age. This must be supplied on the assumption that the phrase is elliptical and the term *Jewish* is tacitly understood. Russell and other preterists draw this inference from indications that the end of the age is near and from New Testament references to "the age of the Gentiles."

The Age of the Gentiles

Since the New Testament does speak of the age of the Gentiles, it is reasonable to assume that this age is in contrast to some age of the Jews, since the context makes a sharp contrast between Jews and Gentiles.

We first meet the concept of the age of the Gentiles in Luke's version of the Olivet Discourse, when Jesus describes the destruction of Jerusalem:

> "But when you see Jerusalem surrounded by armies, then know that its desolation is near. Then let those in Judea flee to the mountains, let those who are in the midst of her depart, and let not those who are in the country enter her. For these are the days of vengeance, that all things which are written may be fulfilled. But woe to those who are pregnant and to those who are nursing babies in those days! For there will be great distress in the land and wrath upon this people. And they will fall by the edge of the sword, and

be led away captive into all nations. And Jerusalem will be trampled by Gentiles until the times of the Gentiles are fulfilled."

(Luke 21:20–24)

Here the times of the Gentiles are related to the occupation of Jerusalem by non-Jewish people. But this Gentile occupation of Jerusalem will not endure indefinitely. There is a crucial "until" mentioned here. This word fixes a temporal point of completion. This text figured prominently in eschatological expectations that were rekindled in 1967 when Jews wrested control of Jerusalem from the Arab Gentiles who had controlled it.

In Luke's account of the Olivet Discourse, the description of the parousia follows immediately upon verse 24. This raises the question: Will the parousia described here take place *after* the times of the Gentiles are fulfilled, i.e. after Jerusalem is restored to the Jews? Or does Luke 21:27 refer to a parousia that signals the end of one age or time (the age of the Jews) and the beginning of a new one, the times of the Gentiles?

Various schemas have been offered. One is that the Jewish dispensation was temporarily halted in A.D. 70, followed by an interim during which the focus is on the mission to the Gentiles, followed by the renewal of Jewish redemption at the end of time. Another is that all Christian history between the fall of Jerusalem and the parousia of Christ is the times of the Gentiles. And a third is that the times of the Gentiles was the very short span of time between the beginning of the siege of Jerusalem and the city's destruction.

Luke's reference to "the times of the Gentiles" lends credence to the idea that Scripture distinguishes between a Jewish epoch and a Gentile epoch. This in turn supports the idea that "the end of the age" may refer to the end of the *Jewish* age.

The Last Days

According to preterists "the last days" refers to the time between the advent of John the Baptist and the destruction of

Table 3.2

The Nearness of the Last Days
to the Apostles

The Gospels

Matt. 10:23	You [the twelve] will not have gone through the cities of Israel before the Son of Man comes.
Matt. 26:64	You [the high priest] will see the Son of Man coming on the clouds of heaven.

Paul's Letters

Rom. 13:11–12	Now it is high time to awake out of sleep. . . . The night is far spent, the day is at hand.
1 Cor. 7:31	The form of this world is passing away.
1 Cor. 10:11	On [us] . . . the ends of the ages have come.
Phil. 4:5	The Lord is at hand.

General Letters

James 5:8–9	The coming of the Lord is at hand. . . . Behold, the Judge is standing at the door.
1 Peter 4:7	The end of all things is at hand.
1 John 2:18	It is the last hour . . . we know that it is the last hour.

**The Book of
Revelation**

1:1	The Revelation of Jesus Christ . . . [shows the] things which must shortly take place.
1:3	The time is near.
3:11	Behold, I come quickly!
22:6–7	His [the Lord God's] angel . . . [showed] His servants the things which must shortly take place. Behold, I am coming quickly.
22:10	The time is at hand.
22:12	Behold, I am coming quickly.
22:20	Surely I am coming quickly.

Jerusalem. This "eschaton" refers not to a time in the distant future, but to a time that is imminent. Gary DeMar summarizes the relevant passages of the New Testament with emphasis on the radical nearness of the events predicted:

> Some cataclysmic event was on the horizon, and the first-century church was being warned to prepare for it. There is no getting around this language and the ultimate conclusion that many of the verses that many believe are yet to be fulfilled have been fulfilled. . . .
> 1. "And you will be hated by all on account of My name, but it is the one who has endured to the end who will be saved. But whenever they persecute you in this city, flee to the next; *for truly I say to you, you shall not finish going through the cities of Israel until the Son of Man comes.*" (Matthew 10:22–23, emphasis added)
> 2. "Jesus said to [the high priest], 'You have said it yourself [that I am the Christ, the Son of God]; nevertheless I tell you, hereafter *you shall see the Son of Man sitting at the right*

hand of power, and coming on the clouds of heaven'" (Matthew 26:64, emphasis added).

3. "And this do, knowing the time, that it is already the hour for you to awaken from sleep; for now salvation is nearer to us than when we believed" (Romans 13:11).

4. *"The night is almost gone and the day is at hand.* Let us therefore lay aside the deeds of darkness and put on the armor of light." (Romans 13:12, emphasis added)

5. "For the form of this world *is passing away"* (1 Corinthians 7:31, emphasis added).

6. "Now these things happened to [Israel] as an example, and they were written for our instruction, *upon whom the ends of the ages have come"* (1 Corinthians 10:11, emphasis added).

7. "Let your forbearing spirit be known to all men. *The Lord is near."* (Philippians 4:5, emphasis added)

8. *"The end of all things is at hand;* therefore be of sound judgment and sober spirit for the purpose of prayer" (1 Peter 4:7, emphasis added).

9. "You too be patient; strengthen your hearts, *for the coming of the Lord is at hand.* Do not complain, brethren, against one another, that you yourselves may not be judged; behold, *the Judge is standing right at the door."* (James 5:8–9, emphasis added)

10. "Children, *it is the last hour;* and just as you have heard that antichrist is coming, even now many antichrists have arisen; from this *we know that it is the last hour"* (1 John 2:18, emphasis added).

11. "The Revelation of Jesus Christ, which God gave Him to show to His bond-servants, *the things which must shortly take place. . . ."* (Revelation 1:1, emphasis added)

12. "Blessed is he who reads and those who hear the words of the prophecy, and heed the things which are written in it; *for the time is near"* (Revelation 1:3, emphasis added).

13. *"I am coming quickly;* hold fast what you have, in order that no one take your crown" (Revelation 3:11).

14. "And he said to me, 'These words are faithful and true'; and the Lord, the God of the spirits of the prophets, sent His angel to show his bond-servants *the things which must shortly take place"* (Revelation 22:6, emphasis added).

15. "And behold, *I am coming quickly.* Blessed is he who heeds the words of the prophecy of this book" (Revelation 22:7, emphasis added).

16. "And he said to me, 'Do not seal up the words of the prophecy of this book, *for the time is near"* (Revelation 22:10, emphasis added). Compare this verse with Daniel 12:4, where Daniel is told to "seal up the book until the end of time."

17. "Behold, *I am coming quickly,* and My reward is with Me, to render to every man according to what he has done" (Revelation 22:12, emphasis added; cf. Matthew 16:27).

18. "He who testifies to these things says, 'Yes, *I am coming quickly.'* Amen. Come, Lord Jesus." (Revelation 22:20, emphasis added)

These passages and many others like them tell us that a significant eschatological event was to occur in the lifetime of those who heard and read the prophecies.[9]

The passages listed by DeMar are among those that have led higher-critical scholars to be skeptical of the New Testament and to see within it attempts to adjust the narrative to account for unfulfilled prophecies and parousia-delay. When such passages are grouped together as DeMar has done, they strongly suggest a near-time fulfillment. Some of them can be handled more easily than others. For example number 2 (Matt. 26:64), which gives Jesus' words to Caiaphas, may refer to an indefinite future. Caiaphas's "seeing" the coming of Christ in the "hereafter" does not demand a first-century fulfillment.

One of the most crucial passages cited above, however, is that found in number 6 (1 Cor. 10:11). Here is mentioned "the ends of the ages" that have come upon the Jews. This text supports the thesis that "the end of the age" means "the end of the Jewish age." Russell places strong emphasis on this text:

> The phrase "the end of the ages" *[ta teleμ tomn aiom nom n]* is equivalent to "the end of the age" *[eμ sunteleia tou aiom nos],* and "the end" *[to telos].* They all refer to the same period, viz. the close of the Jewish age, or dispensation, which was now at hand. . . .

It is sometimes said that the whole period between the incarnation and the end of the world is regarded in the New Testament as "the end of the age." But this bears a manifest incongruity in its very front. How could the *end* of a period be a long protracted duration? Especially how could it be longer than the period of which it is the end? More time has already elapsed since the incarnation than from the giving of the law to the first coming of Christ: so that, on this hypothesis, the end of the age is a great deal longer than the age itself.[10]

You turned to God from idols
to serve the living and true God,
and to wait for His Son
from heaven. . . .

(1 Thess. 1:9–10)

4

What Did Paul Teach in His Letters?

J. Stuart Russell begins his treatment of the Epistles by giving attention to the Thessalonian correspondence. He first treats 1 Thessalonians 1:9–10: "For they themselves declare concerning us what manner of entry we had to you, and how you turned to God from idols to serve the living and true God, and to wait for His Son from heaven, whom He raised from the dead, even Jesus who delivers us from the wrath to come." This verse accentuates two critical motifs of the New Testament: the church's waiting for Christ and Christ's deliverance of his people "from the wrath to come."

Russell sees a link between Paul's reference to "the wrath to come" and John the Baptist's warning to his generation to "flee from the wrath to come" (Luke 3:7). "It would be a mistake to suppose," Russell says, "that St. Paul here refers to the retribution which awaits every sinful soul in a future state; it was a particu-

Wrath in 1 Thessalonians 1–2	
Future Wrath (1:10)	Present Wrath (2:16)
Jesus . . . delivers us [followers of the Lord] from the wrath to come.	Wrath has come upon them [the Jews] to the uttermost.

lar and predicted catastrophe which he had in view. 'The coming wrath' [hē orgē hē erchomenē] of this passage is identical with the 'coming wrath' [orgē mellousa] of the second Elijah; it is identical with 'the days of vengeance,' and 'wrath upon this people,' predicted by our Lord (Luke 21:23). It is 'the day of wrath, and revelation of the righteous judgment of God,' spoken of by St. Paul (Rom. 2:5)."[1]

In 1 Thessalonians 2:16 Paul writes, ". . . [the Jews are] forbidding us to speak to the Gentiles that they may be saved, so as always to fill up the measure of their sins; but wrath has come upon them to the uttermost." This verse, when placed next to Paul's statement in chapter 1, is somewhat confusing. In the first chapter the wrath is future, while in this chapter the wrath has already come.

John Calvin says of this: "[Paul] means that they have absolutely no hope, because they are the vessels of the wrath of the Lord. What he is saying is that the just vengeance of God besets and harries them, and will not leave them until they perish."[2]

Jonathan Edwards preached a sermon on 1 Thessalonians 2:16 entitled *When the Wicked Shall Have Filled Up the Measure of Their Sin, Wrath Will Come upon Them to the Uttermost*. In this sermon he comments on the significance of the term *uttermost* as it relates to the wrath of God:

> The degree of their punishment, is the *uttermost* degree. This may respect both a national and personal punishment. If we take it as a *national* punishment, a little after the time when the epistle was written, wrath came upon the nation of the Jews to the uttermost, in their terrible destruction by the Romans; when, as Christ said, "was great tribulation, such as never was since the beginning of the world to that time" (Matt. 24:21). That nation had before suffered many of the fruits of divine wrath for their sins; but this was

beyond all, this was their highest degree of punishment as a nation. . . . By this expression is also denoted the *certainty* of this punishment. For though the punishment was then future, yet it is spoken of as present: "The wrath *is* come upon them to the uttermost." It was as certain as if it had already taken place. . . . It also denotes the *near approach* of it. *Thy wrath* IS *come;* i.e. it is just at hand; it is at the door; as it proved with respect to that nation; their terrible destruction by the Romans was soon after the apostle wrote this epistle.[3]

In this manner Edwards ties together "the wrath to come" of chapter 1 with the "wrath [that] has come upon them" in chapter 2.

Also in chapter 2, and only three verses later, the apostle speaks of the parousia of Christ: "For what is our hope, or joy, or crown of rejoicing? Is it not even you in the presence of our Lord Jesus Christ at His coming?" (1 Thess. 2:19)

In the close conjunction of these two events, the coming of the uttermost wrath and the coming of Christ, Russell sees a reference to the predicted event that will be fatal to the enemies of Christ and a joyous victory for his friends. "Everywhere the most malignant opposers and persecutors of Christianity were the Jews," writes Russell. "The annihilation of the Jewish nationality, therefore, removed the most formidable antagonist of the Gospel and brought rest and relief to suffering Christians. Our Lord had said to His disciples, when speaking of this approaching catastrophe, 'When these things begin to come to pass, then look up, and lift up your heads, for your redemption draweth nigh' (Luke 21:28)."[4]

At first glance Russell's comments may appear to be anti-Semitic. But the reality in the first century was that the most intense persecution of the Christian church came, not from the Romans, but from the Jewish community. The Romans and the outside world viewed the Christian community as merely a small sect of Judaism. Christianity did not spread globally and become a world religious force until after Jerusalem was destroyed and the Jewish people were scattered among the nations. The same apostle who speaks of "the wrath to come" was anything but anti-Semitic, as becomes clear when he says he would be willing to perish himself if it would mean the redemption of his "kinsmen according to the flesh," the Israelites (Rom. 9:3).

The Thessalonian correspondence figures heavily in biblical eschatology, particularly because of its description of the rapture (1 Thess. 4:17) and of the coming of "the man of sin" or "the lawless one" (2 Thess. 2:3–10). These themes, which are vitally important to Russell and preterism, we will pass over for now, but will analyze later.

Eagerly Awaiting the Lord

Russell next treats the references to the parousia in the Corinthian letters. He refers first to 1 Corinthians 1:7–8, where Paul thanks God that the Corinthian believers will "come short in no gift, eagerly waiting for the revelation of our Lord Jesus Christ, who will also confirm you to the end, that you may be blameless in the day of our Lord Jesus Christ."

Paul describes the Corinthian believers as "eagerly waiting" for Christ's coming. If Paul wrote 1 Corinthians around A.D. 57, it is remarkable that, thirteen years before the destruction of Jerusalem, the early Christians were in a posture of eager anticipation. This theme is underlined in red by higher critics. They see in the New Testament writers a strong conviction that Christ would come in the near term, an expectation based on false hopes, hopes that failed to materialize as the years passed. According to these critics this failure required that the church revise its original eschatological hopes.

Russell notes that the Greek translated "eagerly waiting" is also used in Romans 8:19: "For the earnest expectation of the creation *eagerly waits* for the revealing of the sons of God." Luke employs it also to describe Simeon's sense of expectancy as he awaited the Consolation of Israel (Luke 2:25).

Russell sees in this attitude a clear indication that New Testament believers thought the Lord's coming, his parousia, was near. Otherwise, their eager anticipation would most surely end in disappointment.

In this same passage (1 Cor. 1:7–8) Paul refers to "the end." "Obviously, by '*the end*' the apostle does not mean the '*end of life*,'"Russell says. "It is not a general sentiment such as we express when we speak of being '*true to the last*'; it has a definite meaning, and refers to a particular time. It is 'the end' *[to telos]* spoken of by our Lord in His prophetic discourse on the Mount of Olives (Matt. 24:6, 13, 14). It is "the end of the age" *[sunteleia tou aiōnos]* of Matt. 13:40, 49. It is "the end" (1 Cor. 15:24). . . . All these forms of expression refer to the same epoch—viz., the close of the aeon or Jewish age, i.e. the Mosaic dispensation."[5]

Similarly in 1 Corinthians 3 Paul refers to the coming "day": ". . . each one's work will become manifest [clear]; for the Day will declare it, because it will be revealed by fire; and the fire will test each one's work, of what sort it is. If anyone's work which he has built on it endures, he will receive a reward. If anyone's work is burned, he will suffer loss; but he himself will be saved, yet so as through fire." (1 Cor. 3:13–15)

In this passage Paul mentions again "the Day." Already in chapter 1 Paul had spoken of waiting for the day of the Lord. In chapter 3 he describes the manifestations that will accompany this day and uses the image of fire. The day would be a kind of crucible, an ordeal of testing by fire. It is clear that this day is synonymous with the day of the Lord that is linked to the parousia of Christ. The reference to fire has been taken in both a metaphorical and a literal sense. Russell points to the literal burning of Jerusalem as fulfillment of this.

Later, in chapter 7, Paul provides another time-frame reference: ". . . the time is short, so that from now on even those who have wives should be as though they had none, those who weep as though they did not weep, those who rejoice as though they did not rejoice, those who buy as though they did not possess, and those who use this world as not misusing it. For the form of this world is passing away." (1 Cor. 7:29–31)

Paul declares that "the time is short," so short that his readers should live in a style befitting an emergency or crisis situation. Calvin and others see this as a compression of time between the first advent of Christ and his still future second advent. This is the interim of the last days.

The problem with this traditional view is the term *short*. This word can define duration of time or length of space. In both cases it is a relative term. We may ask, "Short compared to what?" Forty years is a short time compared with 2,000 years. Yet 2,000 years is a short time compared with 15 million years. When one announces to people that an event will take place within a short time, however, they would hardly understand that to mean a period of millennia. Surely the Corinthians would not have understood Paul to be urging them to do something because the time is short when in fact it is thousands of years away.

In chapter 10 Paul speaks again of the end: "Now all these things happened to them [all our fathers] as examples, and they were written for our admonition, on whom the ends of the ages have come" (1 Cor. 10:11).

Here the apostle speaks of "the ends of the ages" as having come upon the Jews. Russell sees this as one more reference to the close of the Jewish age. "It is sometimes said that the whole period between the incarnation and the end of the world is regarded in the New Testament as 'the end of the age,'" Russell writes. "But this bears a manifest incongruity in its very front. How could the *end* of a period . . . be longer than the period of which it is the end?"[6]

Later in 1 Corinthians Paul treats the resurrection of the saints, which is also so important to Christian eschatology that I will discuss it separately later. For now we will continue a brief excursion of relevant passages in the Epistles regarding the time-frame of the coming judgment.

Treasuring Up Wrath

In Paul's Epistle to the Romans, we find two important references to the day of the Lord in chapter 2:

Or do you despise the riches of His goodness, forbearance, and longsuffering, not knowing that the goodness of God leads you to repentance? But in accordance with your hardness and your impenitent heart you are treasuring up for yourself wrath in the day of wrath and revelation of the righteous judgment of God, who "will render to each one according to his deeds." . . .

(Rom. 2:4–6)

. . . in the day when God will judge the secrets of men by Jesus Christ, according to my gospel.

(Rom. 2:16)

Paul refers to "the day of wrath" and "the day when God will judge the secrets of men." Presumably both references are to the same "day." Traditionalists see them as references to the yet future last judgment. Preterists like Russell interpret these references as they do all other references to the day of the Lord: this is the dark day of judgment that befell Israel in the destruction of Jerusalem.

Though the above texts lack time-frame references, they may reasonably be linked to later references Paul makes in the same epistle: "And do this, knowing the time, that now it is high time to awake out of sleep; for now our salvation is nearer than when we first believed. The night is far spent, the day is at hand. Therefore let us cast off the works of darkness, and let us put on the armor of light." (Rom. 13:11–12)

This passage is somewhat enigmatic. Paul assumes that his readers know the time. Charles Hodge understands this to mean simply that the readers understood something of the significance of the redemptive-historical time in which they lived. Paul then gives a wake-up call based on the relative nearness of salvation—it was nearer than when they first believed.

Hodge provides three alternative interpretations of this passage:

> . . . The first is, that it means that the time of salvation, or special favour to the Gentiles, and of the destruction of the Jews, was fast approaching. . . . But for this there is no foundation in the simple meaning of the words, nor in the context. Paul evidently refers to something of more general and permanent interest than the overthrow of the Jewish nation, and the consequent freedom of the Gentile converts from their persecutions. The night that was far spent, was not the night of sorrow arising from Jewish bigotry;

and the day that was at hand was something brighter and better than deliverance from its power. A second interpretation . . . is, that the reference is to the second advent of Christ. It is assumed that the early Christians, and even the inspired apostles, were under the constant impression that Christ was to appear in person for the establishment of his kingdom, before that generation passed away. . . .

The third and most common, as well as the most natural interpretation of this passage is, that Paul meant simply to remind them that the time of deliverance was near. . . . The *salvation*, therefore, here intended, is the consummation of the work of Christ in their deliverance from this present evil world, and introduction into the purity and blessedness of heaven.[7]

Of his three options, Hodge favors the third: the nearness of the believers to entering into their heavenly rest. His first two options, which he sharply differentiates, are combined by preterists. The difficulty with the third option is that Paul does not ordinarily speak of redemptive "time" in this manner. Hodge is concerned about the problems faced in options 1 and 2 of unfulfilled prophecy, and this almost forces him to choose option 3.

C. K. Barrett takes a different view:

. . . Like "time," "hour" is an eschatological term, though it is not characteristic of Paul. . . . "Sleep" too is a metaphor which often occurs in eschatological admonitions (e.g. 1 Thess. 5:6–10). Men who live on the edge of the Age to Come cannot afford to relax their vigilance. . . . but Paul is not thinking of salvation in a pietistic way as something that happens to *us* in *our* experience, but as a universal eschatological event. The lapse of time between the conversion of Paul and of his readers and the moment of writing is a significant proportion of the total interval between the resurrection of Jesus and his *parousia* at the last day. . . .

Paul means that this age has almost run its course, and that accordingly the Age to Come must very soon dawn.[8]

Russell canvases other New Testament Epistles. He cites two references in Paul's Letter to the Colossians: "When Christ who is our life appears, then you also will appear with Him in glory.

... Because of these things the wrath of God is coming upon the sons of disobedience. ..." (Col. 3:4, 6)

Russell sees a link between these texts in Colossians and Paul's teaching in Romans 8:19 regarding the glory that is about to be revealed. He sees this as an allusion to the same event and the same time-period. Again the contrast is mentioned between the coming glory of the people of God and the coming wrath on the enemies of God.

Gathering Together All Things

Then Russell turns his attention to Paul's Letter to the Ephesians:

> In Him we have redemption through His blood, the forgiveness of sins, according to the riches of His grace which He made to abound toward us in all wisdom and prudence, having made known to us the mystery of His will, according to His good pleasure which He purposed in Himself, that in the dispensation of the fullness of the times He might gather together in one all things in Christ, both which are in heaven and which are on earth. ...
>
> *(Eph. 1:7–10)*

Two elements of this passage relate to the issue at hand. The first element is the term *mystery*. This term, a favorite of Paul's, refers to that which once was hidden but is now being revealed. The chief mystery of which he speaks (particularly in Colossians) is the inclusion of the Gentiles in the body of Christ. The second element is Paul's reference to "the dispensation of the fullness of the times." The term *dispensation* may be translated here "economy." This economy is related to "the fullness of the times" and includes the gathering together in one all things in Christ. Russell says of this:

> He saw the barriers of separation between Jew and Gentile, the antipathies of races, "the middle wall of partition," broken down by Christ, and one great family or brotherhood formed out of all nations, and kindreds, and peoples, and tongues, under the all-

reconciling and uniting power of the atoning blood. We cannot be mistaken, then, in understanding this mystery of the "gathering together in one of all things in Christ" as the same which is more fully explained in chap. 3:5, 6, "the mystery which in other ages was not made known unto the sons of men, as it is now revealed unto his holy apostles and prophets by the Spirit; that the Gentiles should be fellow-heirs, and of the same body, and partakers of his promise in Christ by the gospel." This is the *unification*, "the summing up," or consummation, to which the apostle makes such frequent reference in this epistle. . . .[9]

C. Leslie Mitton comments on Ephesians 1:7–10 that the plan for the fullness of time is a strategy carefully designed by God and rooted in his eternal plan. "It was something which God had long intended," Mitton says, "something he waited to implement at that precise moment when Christ's presence on earth would prove to be most timely and effective. . . . He would come when the time was just opportune for him to make the maximum impact. . . . Greek had more than one word for 'time.' The word used here is one which would not be used for a vague period of time, a merely uneventful accumulation of minutes, hours and days, but rather for some 'time' or moment of intense significance."[10]

Mitton sees the link between these words and the words of Jesus in Mark 1:15: "The time is fulfilled." Russell sees it as a reference to "the regeneration" or times of refreshing mentioned in Matthew 19:28 and "the times of restoration" mentioned in Acts 3:21. Russell argues that all of these events take place at the close of the Jewish age. He cites the observation of W. J. Conybeare and J. S. Howson concerning "the ages to come" mentioned in Ephesians 2:7: "'*In the ages which are coming*'; viz. the time of Christ's perfect triumph over evil, always contemplated in the New Testament as *near at hand*."[11]

References to the parousia in the Pastoral Epistles are numerous. Russell's list of these references to the last times is reproduced in table 4.1. Russell concludes that all of these verses refer to the same period or time. All either assume or directly affirm that their time-frame is not far distant, that they must occur

Table 4.1

References to the Last Times

The End of the Age

Matt. 13:39	The harvest is the end of the age.
Matt. 13:40	So it will be at the end of this age.
Matt. 13:49	So it will be at the end of the age.
Matt. 24:3	What will be the sign of Your coming, and of the end of the age?
Matt. 28:20	I am with you always, even to the end of the age.
Heb. 9:26	But now, once at the end of the ages, He has appeared.

The End

Matt. 10:22	He who endures to the end will be saved.
Matt. 24:6	But the end is not yet.
Matt. 24:13	He who endures to the end shall be saved.
Matt. 24:14	Then the end will come.
1 Cor. 1:8	Who will also confirm you to the end.
1 Cor. 10:11	On whom the ends of the ages have come.
1 Cor. 15:24	Then comes the end.
Heb. 3:6	Firm to the end.
Heb. 3:14	Hold the beginning of our confidence steadfast to the end.
Heb. 6:11	Show the same diligence . . . until the end.
1 Peter 4:7	The end of all things is at hand.
Rev. 2:26	He who . . . keeps My works until the end.

The Last Times, Days, etc.

1 Tim. 4:1	In latter times some will depart from the faith.
2 Tim. 3:1	In the last days perilous times will come.
Heb. 1:2	[God] has in these last days spoken to us.
James 5:3	You have heaped up treasure in the last days.
1 Peter 1:5	Salvation ready to be revealed in the last time.
1 Peter 1:20	[Who] was manifest in these last times for you.
2 Peter 3:3	Scoffers will come in the last days.
1 John 2:18	It is the last hour.
Jude 18	That there would be mockers in the last time.

The Day

Matt. 25:13	You know neither the day nor the hour in which the Son of man is coming.
Luke 17:30	The day when the Son of Man is revealed.
Rom. 2:16	In the day when God will judge the secrets of men.
1 Cor. 3:13	The day will declare it.
Heb. 10:25	You see the Day approaching.

That Day

Matt. 7:22	Many will say to Me in that day, "Lord, Lord."
Matt. 24:36	But of that day and hour no one knows.

Continued

Luke 10:12	It will be more tolerable in that Day for Sodom.
Luke 21:34	That day comes on you unexpectedly.
1 Thess. 5:4	That this Day should overtake you as a thief.
2 Thess. 2:3	That Day will not come unless the falling away comes first.
2 Tim. 1:12	He is able to keep what I have committed to Him until that Day.
2 Tim. 1:18	That he may find mercy from the Lord in that Day.
2 Tim. 4:8	The crown . . . which the Lord . . . will give to me on that Day.

The Day of the Lord
1 Cor. 1:8	That you may be blameless in the day of our Lord Jesus Christ.
1 Cor. 5:5	That his spirit may be saved in the day of the Lord Jesus.
2 Cor. 1:14	You also are ours, in the day of the Lord Jesus.
Phil. 2:16	That I may rejoice in the day of Christ.
1 Thess. 5:2	The day of the Lord so comes as a thief in the night.

The Day of God
| 2 Peter 3:12 | Looking for and hastening the coming of the day of God. |

The Great Day
Acts 2:20	The great and notable day of the Lord.
Jude 6	The judgment of the great day.
Rev. 6:17	The great day of His wrath has come.
Rev. 16:14	The battle of that great day of God Almighty.

The Day of Wrath
| Rom. 2:5 | Treasuring up for yourself wrath in the day of wrath. |
| Rev. 6:17 | The great day of His wrath has come. |

The Day of Judgment
Matt. 10:15	It will be more tolerable . . . in the day of judgment.
Matt. 11:22	It will be more tolerable . . . in the day of judgment.
Matt. 11:24	It shall be more tolerable . . . in the day of judgment.
Matt. 12:36	They will give account of it in the day of judgment.
2 Peter 2:9	To reserve the unjust . . . for the day of judgment.
2 Peter 3:7	The day of judgment and perdition of ungodly men.
1 John 4:17	That we may have boldness in the day of judgment.

The Day of Redemption
| Eph. 4:30 | You were sealed for the day of redemption. |

The Last Day
John 6:39	I should raise it up at the last day.
John 6:40	I will raise him up at the last day.
John 6:44	I will raise him up at the last day.
John 6:54	I will raise him up at the last day.
John 11:24	He will rise again in the resurrection at the last day.

within the life-time of the generation that rejected Christ, and that the destruction of Jerusalem is the close of the age, the end, and the day of the Lord.[12]

Closely connected with the texts that refer to the last days are those that refer to the apostasy that is to come. Russell supplies an even longer catalogue of references to false prophets, false Christs, false teachers, false apostles, deceivers, and so forth. Regarding these references, Russell reaches the following conclusions:

1. That they all refer to the same great defection from the faith, designated by St. Paul "the apostasy."
2. That this apostasy was to be very general and widespread.
3. That it was to be marked by an extreme depravity of morals, particularly by sins of the flesh.
4. That it was to be accompanied by pretensions to miraculous power.
5. That it was largely, if not chiefly, Jewish in its character.
6. That it rejected the incarnation and divinity of the Lord Jesus Christ—*i.e.* was the predicted Antichrist.
7. That it was to reach its full development in the "last times," and was to be the precursor of the Parousia.[13]

Russell notes that the evils Paul warns about in the future are represented by both John and Peter as being actually present.

The author of Hebrews says God has spoken by his Son "in these last days" (1:2). Clearly the passage assigns Jesus' earthly ministry to the "last days." Might the qualifier *these* hint at a distinction between the last days that included the incarnation and some other still-future last days? Regardless such an inference, one thing is certain: Jesus' earthly ministry belonged to some aspect or category of the last days.

Appearing a Second Time

While exploring the rest of the Epistle to the Hebrews, we note some important texts, particularly in chapters 9–10.

Therefore it was necessary that the copies of the things in the heavens should be purified with these, but the heavenly things themselves with better sacrifices than these. For Christ has not entered the holy places made with hands, which are copies of the true, but into heaven itself, now to appear in the presence of God for us; not that He should offer Himself often, as the high priest enters the Most Holy Place every year with blood of another—He then would have had to suffer often since the foundation of the world; but now, once at the end of the ages, He has appeared to put away sin by the sacrifice of Himself. And as it is appointed for men to die once, but after this the judgment, so Christ was offered once to bear the sins of many. To those who eagerly wait for Him He will appear a second time, apart from sin, for salvation.

(Heb. 9:23–28)

This passage refers to both the first and second appearances of Christ. The context for his first appearance is "the end of the ages." Yet his followers are still waiting for him to appear a second time. Simon J. Kistemaker comments: "When did Christ come? The author of Hebrews writes, 'at the end of the ages.' This does not have to refer to the end of time, because in the same context the writer says that Christ will appear a second time (v. 28). The expression apparently points to the total impact of Christ's coming and the effect of his atoning work. And because of his triumph over sin, we live in the last age."[14]

This exposition is a bit curious. Kistemaker draws the conclusion that the expression "end of the ages" need not refer to the end of time. This seems to be more than a mild understatement. If Christ's first coming at "the end of the ages" has already occurred and if considerable time has elapsed since that coming, then it is impossible to identify "the end of the ages" with the end of time. If the second appearing of Christ here refers to his judgment on Jerusalem, it would still fit in the framework of "the end of the ages" that is not the end of all time. If the second coming refers to Jesus' coming at the end of time, then we must distinguish between two different "last times." Or we must compress the time that has elapsed since the atonement into a lengthy

interim of last times and consider our present time as a contin-
uation of the last age, as Kistemaker apparently does.

Philip Edgcumbe Hughes treats the passage in similar fashion:
"All that preceded the advent of Christ was leading up to this cli-
mactic event which is the focal point for the true perspective of
all human history. With his coming the long years of desire and
expectation are ended and the last, the eschatological, era of the
present world is inaugurated (cf. Heb. 1:2). Consequently, we who
live since his coming are those 'upon whom the end of the age
has come' (1 Cor. 10:11)."[15]

In the very next chapter of Hebrews, the author speaks of the
"Day approaching":

> Therefore, brethren, having boldness to enter the Holiest by the
> blood of Jesus, by a new and living way which He consecrated for
> us, through the veil, that is, His flesh, and having a High Priest over
> the house of God, let us draw near with a true heart in full assur-
> ance of faith, having our hearts sprinkled from an evil conscience
> and our bodies washed with pure water. Let us hold fast the con-
> fession of our hope without wavering, for He who promised is
> faithful. And let us consider one another in order to stir up love
> and good works, not forsaking the assembling of ourselves
> together, as is the manner of some, but exhorting one another,
> and so much the more as you see the Day approaching.
>
> *(Heb. 10:19–25)*

This text includes an exhortation that follows the teaching of
the perfect sacrifice of Christ. The exhortation is intensified in
light of the reader's vision of the approaching day. Russell, of
course, sees this as a reference to the nearness of Jerusalem's
destruction and all that this entails. The nearness of Christ's coming is reinforced in verse 37: "For yet a little while, and He who is
coming will come and will not tarry" (Heb. 10:37).

It is difficult to escape the conclusion that the author of
Hebrews links the approaching day with the coming of Christ
and says that both are close at hand. Hughes treats this in the following manner:

When spoken of in this absolute manner, "the Day" can mean only the last day, that ultimate eschatological day, which is the day of reckoning and judgment, known as the Day of the Lord. . . . Many have suggested that there may be a more proximate reference by our author to the impending destruction of Jerusalem and with it of the old order of things (A.D. 70), in addition to the eschatological connotation of the term. . . . While, however, the events of A.D. 70 were invested with the most portentous significance (cf. Matt. 24), and in the prophetic perspective there could be lesser "days of the Lord" which pointed to the certainty of the ultimate day of judgment, "the Day," without any qualification and therefore emphatic in the absoluteness of its significance, must be the day of Christ's return when this present age will be brought to its conclusion and his everlasting kingdom over the new heaven and the new earth universally established.[16]

Hughes is emphatic that "the Day" refers to the final and consummate day of the Lord. Yet he speaks of "lesser" days of the Lord such as the one in A.D. 70. He feels some of the weight of the language attached to this coming day suggesting its nearness. He writes:

But, it may be objected, if the writer of Hebrews and his readers did indeed believe that this Day was drawing near, its non-arrival would seem to have falsified their expectation. Nearly two millennia have now passed and the Day has not come: can it seriously be regarded as other than a mistaken expectation and a non-event? This, however, is not at all a new problem in the church. . . . Just as the promise of the first coming of Christ, though apparently long delayed in its fulfillment, was proved true by the event, so it will be with the promise concerning the day of his second coming. . . . "The period between the first advent of Christ and His parousia is the end-time, the 'last days,' the 'last hour,'" writes F. F. Bruce. "Whatever the duration of the period may be, for faith 'the time is at hand' (Rev. 1:3). Each successive Christian generation is called upon to live as the generation of the end-time, if it is to live as a *Christian* generation."[17]

This line of reasoning begs the question. If indeed the promise is fulfilled when the event transpires, this does not mean that the promised time-frame is also proven true. When F. F. Bruce speaks of faith making the time be "at hand," this sounds all too much like Rudolf Bultmann's famous theology of timelessness, which removes the object of faith from the realm of real history and consigns it to a supertemporal realm of the always present *hic et nunc*. Russell countered similar theories in his own day. "It is not true that the Parousia 'is always near, and always ready to break forth upon the church,'" he says, "any more than that the birth of Christ, His crucifixion, or His resurrection, is always ready to break forth."[18]

Not one stone shall be left here upon another, that shall not be thrown down.

(Matt. 24:2)

What about the Destruction of Jerusalem?

he New Testament was written in Greek rather than Hebrew. This was the case because Palestine was a geo-political football, tossed to and fro among the world powers of antiquity. This tiny nation, about the size of Maryland and only slightly larger than Vermont, was situated on a land bridge that connected three continents, Europe, Asia, and Africa. Whoever controlled this bridge controlled the trade routes connecting these continents.

Israel experienced conquest and domination by the Egyptians, the Assyrians, the Babylonians, the Persians, the Greeks, and the Romans, to name but a few. The New Testament was written in Greek as a consequence of the military triumphs of Alexander the Great. Alexander was a student of Aristotle. Aristotle's passion for metaphysical and scientific unity was translated by his most illustrious pupil into a passion for cultural unity. Part of his zeal in military conquest was to export Greek culture to the entire Mediterranean world.

At the close of the Old Testament period, Palestine was under the control of the Persian Empire. In the fourth century B.C. Alexander conquered the Persians. He also went to Egypt and established the city of Alexandria (331), which became a center of Hellenistic philosophy and culture. In 323 Alexander marched to Babylon, where he contracted a fever and died at age 32. His kingdom was divided among his generals, the most important of whom produced the Ptolemaic dynasty in Egypt and the Seleucid dynasty in Syria and the east. Palestine was annexed to Egypt by Ptolemy I in 320 B.C. This regime allowed the Jewish people to practice their religion freely. In 198 B.C. Antiochus III of the Seleucid dynasty wrested control of Palestine from the Ptolemies and annexed it to Syria. The Seleucids embarked on a systematic program of Hellenizing Palestine.

In 175 B.C. the Hellenization process reached its apex (or nadir) under Antiochus Epiphanes, who captured Jerusalem, plundered the temple, and massacred many of its citizens. He outlawed observance of the Sabbath, the practice of circumcision, and the possession of the Hebrew Scriptures, declaring all three to be capital crimes. These extreme measures gave rise to the Maccabean revolt, which finally led to freedom in 142 B.C. This freedom endured until Palestine was once more conquered by a foreign power. Palestine was subjugated by the Romans in 63 B.C.

Though the New Testament was written in the Greek language, it was written during a period of Roman dominion. Jesus was born during the reign of Caesar Augustus and lived when the Roman official Pontius Pilate was procurator. The history of the New Testament era is intertwined with the history of the Roman Empire.

In the roots of these intertwining histories, there is an irony. The Prophet Isaiah was called in the year that King Uzziah died (Isa. 6:1–13). That year has been cited as 758 B.C. "It was in this year that Israel as a people was given up to hardness of heart, and as a kingdom and country to devastation and annihilation by the imperial power of the world," Franz Delitzsch writes. "How significant a fact, as Jerome observes in connection with this passage, that the year of Uzziah's death should be the year in which Romulus was born; and that it was only a short time after the death of Uzziah (viz. 754 B.C. according to Varro's chronology) that Rome itself was founded! The national glory of Israel died out with king Uzziah, and has never revived to this day."[1]

According to some interpreters of the Old Testament, the Prophet Daniel predicted the dominion of the Roman Empire in his interpretation of Nebuchadnezzar's dream of the colossus (Dan. 4:19–27). Some see the four empires denoted there as those of Babylon, Medo-Persia, Greece, and Rome.[2]

Palestine came under Roman dominion in 63 B.C. when Pompey took possession of Jerusalem. Pompey is famous in Western history for being part of the First Triumvirate in 60 B.C. with Julius Caesar and Crassus. After dissension developed among the three, Caesar emerged as the dictator. In William Shakespeare's *Julius Caesar*, Caesar, assassinated in the Roman Forum by Brutus, falls dead at the foot of the bust of Pompey.

With Pompey's conquest of Jerusalem, the Jewish kingship was abolished and Judea was required to pay tribute to Rome. For a time the Jews were allowed to have native rulers. During the reign of Julius Caesar, concessions were made to the Jews regarding taxation and exemption from military service. Caesar named Antipater, an Idumean ruler, as procurator of the Jewish nation. After the death of Caesar, the Second Triumvirate was formed by Mark Anthony (of Anthony and Cleopatra fame), Octavian (who later became Caesar Augustus), and Lepidus.

In 27 B.C. Octavian became the first emperor of Rome, and he reigned until his death in A.D. 14. He was succeeded by his adopted son Tiberius, who reigned until A.D. 37. Tiberius was followed by the notorious Caligula, who held power until he was assassinated in A.D. 41. He was followed by Claudius I, who reigned until A.D. 54. Claudius was succeeded by Nero, who ruled from A.D. 54 to 68.

Following the death of Nero, the empire was in upheaval and a power struggle ensued. Nero was succeeded by Galba, who was soon killed and replaced by Otho in A.D. 69. He, in turn, was killed and replaced by Vitellius. Vitellius had the support of the Senate, but not the military. Followers of Vespasian captured Rome, killed Vitellius, and proclaimed Vespasian emperor. Vespasian ruled from A.D. 69 to 79 and was emperor at the time of Jerusalem's destruction.

The Jewish Historian

An eyewitness to Jerusalem's destruction was Flavius Josephus. James L. Price offers the following synopsis of this Jewish historian's life and career:

> Josephus was born at Jerusalem in A.D. 37–38, the first year of the Emperor Caligula's reign. The time of his death is not known, but he outlived Herod Agrippa, for Josephus records the latter's death in A.D. 100. Josephus was the son of a priest. He claimed descent from the Hasmoneans. As a young man he was attracted by the teachings of various parties and sects in Palestine but eventually he joined the popular party, the Pharisees. During the procuratorship of Felix, Josephus went to Rome to obtain the release of some arrested priests. Shortly after his return the Jewish war began. Perhaps the impressions of Roman power which he had gained led Josephus to attempt to thwart the foolish rebellion in Palestine. But he was swept into the maelstrom as a partisan and for a time held a position of military leadership in Galilee. After the Roman victories in this region and his arrest, Josephus sought to mediate between the warring groups. It was not a popular position for he was suspected by the Romans and hated by the Jews. He was able, nonetheless, to observe much of the war at first hand. Afterwards he witnessed the triumphal procession of Titus at Rome. He lived there, until his death, in order to receive citizenship and various privileges, and to write his "apologies." He assumed the family name of the Emperor Vespasian, Flavius.[3]

Josephus wrote four major works: *The Jewish War, The Antiquities of the Jews, The Life of Flavius Josephus,* and *Against Apion.*[4] He was a controversial person, as Price has noted, and was zealous to vindicate both himself as a historian and his people, the Jews. His credibility as a historian was sharply criticized by nineteenth-century scholars. His writings reflect a certain bias at times and a form of self-aggrandizement. He has been charged with exaggerating, particularly the numbers of those slain in various battles and even more particularly the number of people killed in the Romans' conquest of Jerusalem. Yet Josephus provides an invaluable resource for his times, especially as an eyewitness to the fall of Jerusalem. "Without the writings of Josephus, a connected narrative of Jewish history in New Testament times would be impossible," says Price. "Few would deny him a place among the greatest historians of the ancient world."[5]

In his preface to *The Wars of the Jews*, Josephus promises an account that is accurate with respect to both the Roman conquerors and his Jewish countrymen:

> But if any one makes an unjust accusation against us, when we speak so passionately about the tyrants, or the robbers, or sorely bewail the misfortunes of our country, let him indulge my affections herein, though it be contrary to the rules for writing history; because it had so come to pass, that our city Jerusalem had arrived at a higher degree of felicity than any other city under the Roman government, and yet at last fell into the sorest of calamities again. Accordingly it appears to me, that the misfortunes of all men, from the beginning of the world, if they be compared to these of the Jews, are not so considerable as they were; while the authors of them were not foreigners neither. This makes it impossible for me to contain my lamentations. But, if any one be inflexible in his censures of me, let him attribute the facts themselves to the historical part, and the lamentations to the writer himself only.[6]

Josephus was passionately involved in his own account of the Roman conquest of Palestine. He had a profound affection for his people, and he was personally involved in the war itself. The destruction of Jerusalem did not occur overnight but was the final blow in a lengthy series of military expeditions against Palestine. Before the siege of Jerusalem, many battles were fought as the Romans systematically and relentlessly moved across the land like a juggernaut. Josephus's account of many preliminary events reads like a chronicle of fulfilled biblical prophecy. He refers to the rise of false prophets (2.13), a massacre in Jerusalem (2.14), the slaughter of Jews in Alexandria (2.18), and the invasion of Galilee (3.4).

One of Josephus's most fascinating accounts is that of the siege and conquest of the city of Jotapata. He provides vivid insights into the strategies and tactics employed by the Roman military. Josephus himself was the general in charge of defending the city. The Roman attackers were led by Vespasian (who was not yet emperor). Vespasian surrounded the city with his troops and laid siege to it.

Josephus describes the battering ram the Romans used on Jotapata's fortifications:

> The battering ram is a vast beam of wood like the mast of a ship; its fore-part is armed with a thick piece of iron at the head of it, which is so carved as to be like the head of a ram, whence its name is taken. This ram is slung in the air by ropes passing over its middle, and is hung like the balance in a pair of scales from another beam, and braced by strong beams that pass on both sides of it in the nature of a cross. When this ram is pulled backward by a great number of men with united force, and then thrust forward by the same men, with a mighty noise, it batters the walls with that iron part which is prominent; nor is there any tower so strong, or walls so broad, that can resist any more than its first batteries, but all are forced to yield to it at last.[7]

Josephus tells of the Jews' ingenious ploys to thwart the battering-ram attack, such as pouring sacks of chaff that turned aside the thrusts of the ram, and pouring scalding oil on the Roman soldiers operating the ram.

The siege went on for over forty-five days until the Romans broke into Jotapata and slayed its inhabitants. The Romans took captive 1,200 women and children, according to Josephus. During the course of these events, 40,000 were slain. Josephus himself survived by hiding in a deep pit. But he was betrayed and was taken captive. According to his own account, Josephus was spared by Vespasian because of his valiant behavior during the siege.

This led to a long-term personal relationship between Josephus and both Vespasian and his son Titus. This development enabled Josephus to act as a witness to both sides in the ensuing struggle over Jerusalem. In the crisis surrounding his capture,

Josephus claimed to have dreams of prophetic import. His description reveals much of his own self-consciousness regarding the drama of these events:

> Now Josephus was able to give shrewd conjectures about the interpretation of such dreams as have been ambiguously delivered by God. Moreover, he was not unacquainted with the prophecies contained in the sacred books, as being a priest himself, and of the posterity of priests: and just then was he in an ecstasy; and setting before him the tremendous images of the dreams he had lately had, he put up a secret prayer to God, and said, "Since it pleaseth thee, who hast created the Jewish nation, to depress the same, and since all their good fortune is gone over to the Romans; and since thou hast made choice of this soul of mine to foretell what is to come to pass hereafter, I willingly give them my hands, and am content to live. And I protest openly, that I do not go over to the Romans as a deserter of the Jews, but as a minister from thee."[8]

This testimony reveals that Josephus thought of himself as a general, a statesman, a historian, a priest, and a prophet. It also indicates that he saw the hand of Providence in the tragic events unfolding before his very eyes. Throughout his history he indicates that the fortune of the Jews is the direct result of divine chastisement. In book 4 Josephus recounts how certain Edomites desecrated the temple in Jerusalem and how the Zealots fulfilled ancient prophecies:

> These men, therefore, trampled upon all the laws of man, and laughed at the laws of God; and for the oracles of the prophets, they ridiculed them as the tricks of jugglers; yet did these prophets foretell many things concerning [the rewards of] virtue, and [punishments of] vice, which when these zealots violated, they occasioned the fulfilling of those very prophecies belonging to their own country: for there was a certain ancient oracle of those men, that the city should then be taken and the sanctuary burnt, by right of war, when a sedition should invade the Jews, and their own hand should pollute the temple of God. Now, while these zealots did not [quite] disbelieve these predictions, they made themselves the instruments of their accomplishment.[9]

The Roman Attack on the City

Josephus then tells how the invasion was interrupted when the news arrived of the death of Nero. After Vitellius was killed and Vespasian was proclaimed emperor by his troops, Vespasian made a journey to Rome. His son Titus returned to Jerusalem to carry on the war against the Jews. Meanwhile Vespasian released Josephus from his bonds.

In book 5 Josephus provides a vivid description of Jerusalem at the time of the war, giving such details as the size of the walls and the towers. He carefully describes the temple itself and the size of the stones Herod had used in its construction. Some of the stones were forty-five cubits long, five cubits high, and six cubits wide.

In an early attack the Romans cast stones and shot arrows at the city. The barrage of stones fell on the city like hail. Josephus records the Jews' strange response: ". . . they at first watched the coming of the stone, for it was of a white color, and could therefore not only be perceived by the great noise it made, but could be seen also before it came by its brightness; accordingly the watchmen that sat upon the towers gave them notice when the engine was let go, and the stone came from it, and cried out aloud in their own country language, 'THE STONE COMETH'; so those that were in its way stood off, and threw themselves down upon the ground; by which means, and by their thus guarding themselves, the stone fell down and did them no harm."[10]

There is a textual dispute concerning the original wording of the sentence "The stone cometh." Certain manuscripts read "The son cometh." J. Stuart Russell sees great significance in the latter rendition, which is probably original. He writes:

It could not but be well known to the Jews that the great hope and faith of the Christians was the speedy coming of the Son. It was about this very time, according to Hegesippus, that St. James, the brother of our Lord, publicly testified in the temple that "the Son of man was about to come in the clouds of heaven," and then sealed his testimony with his blood. It seems highly probable that the Jews, in their defiant and desperate blasphemy, when they saw the white mass hurtling through the air, raised the ribald cry, "The

Son is coming," in mockery of the Christian hope of the Parousia, to which they might trace a ludicrous resemblance in the strange appearance of the missle.[11]

In book 5 Josephus records his former pleas to his own people to repent of their sins. He saw that their fight was ultimately not against the Romans but against God. "Wherefore I cannot but suppose that God is fled out of his sanctuary, and stands on the side of those against whom you fight," Josephus writes. "Now even a man, if he be but a good man, will fly from an impure house, and will hate those that are in it; and do you persuade yourselves that God will abide with you in your iniquities, who sees all secret things, and hears what is kept most private!"[12]

In castigating the Jews for their sins, Josephus claimed that his own generation was more wicked than any generation before it, an assessment remarkably similar to that of Jesus.

In book 6 Josephus rehearses the horrors that had befallen the inhabitants of Jerusalem during the siege under Titus. Josephus describes a woman who, in the midst of the famine caused by the siege, took her baby who had been sucking at her breast and killed it. She then roasted her own child, ate half of its body, and offered the rest to bystanders. They expressed their utter contempt for her actions and left the scene in a spirit of trembling.

Josephus then describes the Romans burning the temple and placing Jerusalem under the ban: "While the holy house was on fire, every thing was plundered that came to hand, and ten thousand of those that were caught were slain; nor was there a commiseration of any age, or any reverence of gravity; but children and old men, and profane persons, and priests, were all slain in the same manner; so that this war went round all sorts of men, and brought them to destruction. . . ."[13]

Stars, Comets, and Lights

Perhaps the most strange, even bizarre, report in Josephus's narrative is the sightings of heavenly apparitions:

Thus were the miserable people persuaded by these deceivers, and such as belied God himself; while they did not attend, nor give credit, to the signs that were so evident and did so plainly foretell their future desolation; but, like men infatuated, without either eyes to see, or minds to consider, did not regard the denunciations that God made to them. Thus there was a star resembling a sword, which stood over the city, and a comet, that continued a whole year. Thus also, before the Jews' rebellion, and before those commotions which preceded the war, when the people were come in great crowds to the feast of unleavened bread, on the eighth day of the month Xanthicus [Nisan], and at the ninth hour of the night, so great a light shone round the altar and the holy house, that it appeared to be bright day time; which light lasted for half an hour. This light seemed to be a good sign to the unskilful, but was so interpreted by the sacred scribes, as to portend those events that followed immediately upon it. At the same festival also, a heifer, as she was led by the high-priest to be sacrificed, brought forth a lamb in the midst of the temple.[14]

Josephus says these astronomical phenomena triggered false prophecies of hope for Jerusalem and its people. Others have seen in them a different significance. The bright light shining round the temple area may be related to the presence of the Shekina glory, the sign of God's presence. False prophets read it in much the same way that false prophets in Old Testament times viewed the coming day of the Lord—as a time of unqualified weal, a day of pure brightness and glory. They missed the dreadful darkness that would accompany it as a sign of judgment.

The reference to a heifer giving birth to a lamb is bizarre indeed, to the point of raising doubts about Josephus's accuracy as a historian. It is significant, however, that signs in the sky were reported by other historians of events surrounding the destruction of Jerusalem. The Roman historian Tacitus, for example, writes this:

The history on which I am entering is that of a period rich in disasters, terrible with battles, torn by civil struggles, horrible even in peace. Four emperors fell by the sword; there were three civil wars, more foreign wars, and often both at the same time. There was success in the East, misfortune in the West. Illyricum was disturbed, the Gallic provinces wavering, Britain subdued and immediately let go. The Sarmatae and Suebi rose against us; the Dacians won fame by defeats inflicted and suffered; even the Parthians were almost roused to arms through the trickery of a pretended Nero. Moreover, Italy was distressed by disasters unknown before or returning after the lapse of ages. Cities on the rich fertile shores of Campania were swallowed up or overwhelmed; Rome was devastated by conflagrations, in which her most ancient shrines were consumed and the very Capitol fired by citizen's hands. . . . The sea was filled with exiles, its cliffs made foul with the bodies of the dead. In Rome there was more awful cruelty. . . .

Besides the manifold misfortunes that befell mankind, there were prodigies in the sky and on the earth, warnings given by thunderbolts, and prophecies of the future, both joyful and gloomy, uncertain and clear. For never was it more fully proved by awful disasters of the Roman people or by indubitable signs that the gods care not for our safety, but for our punishment.[15]

Though questions might be posed about certain points in Josephus's account of signs in the sky, it is nevertheless clear that some of his testimony is corroborated by others. Perhaps most significant is his reference to the comet that appeared in the sky and remained for a year. Gary DeMar comments:

The appearance of comets in the sky was often taken as a warning of some approaching calamity or a sign of change in existing political structures. . . .
Were there any "signs from heaven" prior to A.D. 70? A comet appeared around A.D. 60 during the reign of Nero. The public speculated that some change in the political scene was imminent: "The historian Tacitus wrote: 'As if Nero were already dethroned, men began to ask who might be his successor.'" Nero took the comet's "threat" seriously. ". . . Nero took no chances as another historian, Suetonius, related: '. . . All children of the condemned men were banished from Rome, and then starved to death or poisoned.' . . . Nero survived that comet by several years. . . ." Then Halley's Comet appeared in A.D. 66. Not long after this Nero committed suicide. Historians have linked the appearance of Halley's Comet, not only

with the death of Nero, but with the destruction of Jerusalem four years later.[16]

In addition to his account of the comet, the sword-like star, and so forth, Josephus provides a most remarkable record of an even more astonishing celestial occurrence, one so extraordinary that the historian himself seems reticent about mentioning it:

> Besides these, a few days after that feast, on the one-and-twentieth day of the month Artemisius [Jyar], a certain prodigious and incredible phenomenon appeared; I suppose the account of it would seem to be a fable, were it not related by those that saw it, and were not the events that followed it of so considerable a nature as to deserve such signals; for, before sun-setting, chariots and troops of soldiers in their armor were seen running about among the clouds, and surrounding of cities. Moreover at that feast which we call Pentecost, as the priests were going by night into the inner [court of the] temple, as their custom was, to perform their sacred ministrations, they said that, in the first place, they felt a quaking, and heard a great noise, and after that they heard a sound as of a great multitude, saying, "Let us remove hence."[17]

Ezekiel's Strange Vision

What is remarkable about this testimony is its similarity to incidents related in the Old Testament. When Ezekiel was a captive in Babylon, he had a vision of the chariot-throne of God. The fearful signs accompanying this theophany included a great sound:

> The likeness of the firmament above the heads of the living creatures was like the color of an awesome crystal, stretched out over their heads. And under the firmament their wings spread out straight, one toward another. Each one had two which covered one side, and each one had two which covered the other side of the body. When they went, I heard the noise of their wings, like the noise of many waters, like the voice of the Almighty, a tumult

Table 5.1

The Judgment on Jerusalem
according to History

Destruction of the temple

Heavenly phenomena

- A star resembling a sword

- A comet (Halley's Comet appeared in A.D. 66)

- A bright light shining around the altar and the temple

- A vision of chariots and soldiers running around among the clouds and surrounding cities

Earthly phenomena (reported by priests)

- A quaking

- A great noise

- The sound of a great multitude saying, "Let us remove hence."

like the noise of an army; and when they stood still, they let down their wings. A voice came from above the firmament that was over their heads; whenever they stood, they let down their wings.

And above the firmament over their heads was the likeness of a throne, in appearance like a sapphire stone; on the likeness of the throne was a likeness with the appearance of a man high above it. Also from the appearance of His waist and upward I saw, as it were, the color of amber with the appearance of fire all around within it; and from the appearance of His waist and downward I saw, as it were, the appearance of fire with brightness all around. Like the appearance of a rainbow in a cloud on a rainy day, so was the appearance of the brightness all around it. This was the appearance of the likeness of the glory of the LORD. So when I saw it, I fell on my face, and I heard a voice of One speaking.

(Ezek. 1:22–28)

The chariot-throne is mentioned again later in the Book of Ezekiel. In chapter 10 Ezekiel saw the chariot-throne with its resplendent glory departing from the temple and from Jerusalem via the East Gate.

> And the cherubim were lifted up. This was the living creature I saw by the River Chebar. When the cherubim went, the wheels went beside them; and when the cherubim lifted their wings to mount up from the earth, the same wheels also did not turn from beside them. When the cherubim stood still, the wheels stood still, and when one was lifted up, the other lifted itself up, for the spirit of the living creature was in them.
>
> Then the glory of the LORD departed from the threshold of the temple and stood over the cherubim. And the cherubim lifted their wings and mounted up from the earth in my sight. When they went out, the wheels were beside them; and they stood at the door of the east gate of the LORD's house, and the glory of the God of Israel was above them.
>
> *(Ezek. 10:15–19)*

Ezekiel's vision was not of the destruction of Jerusalem in A.D. 70, but of the fall of Jerusalem to the Babylonians in 586 B.C. It is significant that this earlier destruction of the holy city was marked by this kind of vision-sign.

Josephus's account of soldiers running around in the clouds also resembles the sight witnessed by Elisha's servant when his eyes were opened to behold the angels that fought for Elisha in Dothan (2 Kings 6:17). These angels were a heavenly army borne by chariots of fire.

Josephus obviously regarded the voice that the priests heard as the voice of God. He announced an imminent departure ("Let us remove hence"), declaring a grim and fatal "Ichabod" to the holy city. (This event was also reported by Tacitus.)

Josephus also mentions dire predictions made in Jerusalem four years earlier by a man who was named, ironically, Jesus. The man repeatedly cried out, "A voice from the east, a voice from the west, a voice from the four winds, a voice against Jerusalem and the holy house, a voice against the bridegrooms and the brides, and a voice against this whole people." This man was taken into custody and beaten with severe stripes. With every stroke of the whip he cried out, "Woe, woe to Jerusalem!"[18]

Josephus concluded his narrative of the destruction of the temple and Jerusalem with this summary: "Now the number of those that were carried captive during this whole war was collected to be ninety-seven thousand; as was the number of those that perished during the whole siege eleven hundred thousand, the greater part of whom were indeed of the same nation [with the citizens of Jerusalem], but not belonging to the city itself; for they were come up from all the country to the feast of unleavened bread, and were on a sudden shut up by an army, which, at the very first, occasioned so great a straitness among them that there came a pestilential destruction upon them, and soon afterward such a famine, as destroyed them more suddenly."[19]

Josephus's record of Jerusalem's fall indicates the radical fulfillment of Jesus' prophecy in the Olivet Discourse. As we have seen, preterists see in this event not only the destruction of the temple and its attending circumstances, but also the parousia of Christ in his judgment-coming. Radical preterists see in this event the fulfillment of all New Testament expectations for the return of Christ and for the last things of eschatology. But here we find sharp disagreement among preterists. Moderate preterists, such as those who hold to a postmillennial view of eschatology, insist that though the bulk of the Olivet Discourse was fulfilled in A.D. 70, there still remains a future coming or parousia of Christ. These views will be considered in the following chapters.

The Revelation of Jesus Christ,
which God gave Him
to show His servants—
things which must shortly
take place. . . .
the time is near.

(Rev. 1:1–3)

What Did John Teach
in Revelation?

Surely no book of the Bible has been studied more closely with regard to the end times than the Book of Revelation, which is sometimes referred to as the New Testament Apocalypse. Because of its arcane literary form, the book has been subjected to a multitude of imaginative and even bizarre interpretations. Some find the genre so puzzling that they despair of ever achieving a sound and consistent interpretation of it. Even John Calvin failed to include it among his prodigious literary output of biblical commentaries.

Many questions torment the interpreter of Revelation. Some suggest that it was written in the style of a drama. Others contend it was written in some form of secret code to prevent hostile authorities from understanding its meaning. Many writers have offered various "keys" to break the code and make its content clear to us today.

More to the point, however, is the crucial question of the book's audience. Was the Revelation written chiefly for the benefit of people living in the final days before the consummation of the kingdom of Christ? Was it written chiefly for the first-century church? Was it written for the church of all ages? These questions are not necessarily mutually exclusive in their scope.

Another crucial issue is the question of the book's meaning. Was it describing events that lie still in the future? Was it describing events that were unfolding in the first century?

Still another question that has been raised afresh in our day is when the Revelation was written. If the book was written in the final decade of the first century (the traditional view), then its prophecies probably do not concern the destruction of Jerusalem, an event that would have already taken place. On the other hand, if Revelation was written before A.D. 70, then a case could be made that it describes chiefly those events leading up to Jerusalem's fall. The when and why questions of the Apocalypse are inseparably bound together.

When probing the meaning of the Book of Revelation, we are immediately faced with a set of problems not unlike those raised by the Olivet Discourse in the Synoptic Gospels. The chief question is once again that of the time-frame references.

The Nearness of the Events

Understanding the time-frame references of Revelation is key to all preterist interpretations of the book. J. Stuart Russell argues that the true key to Revelation is found in its reference to the then contemporary issues it addresses. *"Must it not of necessity refer to matters of contemporary history?"* Russell says. "The only tenable, the only reasonable, hypothesis is that it was intended to be understood by its original readers; but this is as much as to say that it must be occupied with the events and transactions of their own day, and these comprised with a comparatively brief space of time."[1]

Russell's statement sounds somewhat strange. Surely he was aware of the many biblical prophecies of future events that were not fully understood by those living when the prophecies were given. Or one could argue that a future prophecy could be understood by those to whom it was originally given and that they understood that it was indeed a prophecy about the future. Such prophecy would not be useless or irrelevant to the contemporary generation, as every generation of believers is encouraged by God's promises regarding the future.

Russell surely understood this principle and is not arguing simply that, because the Apocalypse was written in the first century, its content must therefore be restricted to events in that time period. Russell indeed seems to argue in this manner. "Yet if the book were meant to unveil the secrets of distant times," he says, "must it not of necessity have been unintelligible to its first readers—and not only unintelligible, but even irrelevant and useless."[2] I think Russell became carried away with his rhetoric at this point and overstated his case. I doubt if he would have made a similar judgment about future prophecies of Isaiah and Jeremiah.

What was really driving Russell at this point was apparently the time-frame references in the Book of Revelation. From these texts Russell attempts to build his case, not from a principle that future prophecy must be relevant to the generation first receiving it. Russell says this about the internal evidence of time-frame:

If there be one thing which more than any other is explicitly and repeatedly affirmed in the Apocalypse it is the *nearness* of the events which it predicts. This is stated, and reiterated again and again, in the beginning, the middle, and the end. We are warned that "the time is *at hand*"; "These things must *shortly* come to pass," "Behold, I come *quickly*"; "Surely I come *quickly*." Yet, in the face of these express and oft-repeated declarations, most interpreters have felt at liberty to ignore the limitations of time altogether, and to roam at will over ages and centuries, regarding the book as a syllabus of church history, an almanac of politico-ecclesiastical events for all Christendom to the end of time. This has been a fatal and inexcusable blunder.[3]

The first time-frame reference occurs in the book's opening verses: "The Revelation of Jesus Christ, which God gave Him to show His servants—things which must shortly take place. And He sent and signified it by His angel to His servant John, who bore witness to the word of God, and to the testimony of Jesus Christ, and to all things that he saw. Blessed is he who reads and those who hear the words of this prophecy, and keep those things which are written in it; for the time is near." (Rev. 1:1–3)

Verse 1 mentions things "which must *shortly* take place." Verse 3 speaks of the time being *near.* These references (and others throughout the book) are handled in various ways by scholars.

The Interpretations of Scholars

George Eldon Ladd writes:

The words "what must soon take place" contain an echo of Daniel 2:28. Although John seldom quoted the Old Testament in a formal way, his book is filled with obvious allusions to the prophetic writings. Here is a fact whose significance many modern critics overlook. . . .

These events are "soon" to "take place." . . . These words have troubled the commentators. The simplest solution is to take the preterist view and to say that John, like the entire early Christian community, thought that the coming of the Lord was near, when in fact they were wrong. Our Lord himself seems to share this error in perspective in the saying: "This generation will not pass away before all these things take place" (Mark 13:30). Others have interpreted the phrase to mean "these events must soon begin"; others "they must certainly begin"; still others, "they must swiftly take place"; that is, once the events begin, the end will come quickly.

However, the simple meaning cannot be avoided. The problem is raised by the fact that the prophets were little interested in chronology, and the future was always viewed as imminent. . . . There is in biblical prophecy a tension between the immediate and the distant future; the distant is viewed through the transparency of the immediate. It is true that the early church lived in expectancy of the return of the Lord, and it is the nature of biblical prophecy to make it possible for every generation to live in expectancy of the end.[4]

To be candid, I find this treatment of the question somewhat disturbing. Ladd grants that "the simplest solution" is the preterist view, but he believes this view drives us to the conclusion that the entire early Christian community, including the Apostle John and our Lord himself, was wrong. Of course this is not the preterist view. The preterist argues, not only that the early church believed the Lord's coming was near (at least with respect to his coming in judgment to Israel), but also that this belief proved to be true.

Ladd grants that this expectation was virtually universal in the early church, but he believes the early church, including Jesus, was "rescued" from a false expectation by the nature of biblical prophecy. Here the question is begged with a vengeance. Did not Jesus and the apostles understand the nature of biblical prophecy? If biblical prophecy is always viewed as imminent, does it not follow that if the prophecies do not occur imminently then the prophecies themselves are false?

I fear I am hearing something that Ladd did not mean to convey. Perhaps the error is in my understanding rather than in his articulation of his point. If the controlling principle is that prophecy is always imminent, then time-frame references would indeed be meaningless.

Ladd's view is echoed to a degree by G. R. Beasley-Murray:

"The time is near," i.e., the time of the fulfillment of the vision disclosed in the revelation. Such is the conviction of all living prophecy, as [Wilhelm] Bousset observed, and not least of all New Testament prophecy (e.g., Rom. 13:11f., 1 Cor. 7:29f., Heb. 10:37, 1 Peter 4:7). A number of factors flow together in this foreshortening—one might call it telescopic—view of history. . . . Accordingly "measuring human affairs with divine measures" (Arethas, cited by [Ernst] Lohmeyer), he sets his day in the context of the last day, and so interprets the issues of his day in the light of the last day. In reality the human measures of time demand that the temporal relationship of John's day to the last day be corrected. Nevertheless John's readers in all times are under the obligation of letting the light of the last day fall on *theirs*, and of relating the issues of their day to the kingdom of God. It is in carrying out that difficult exercise that John's vision ceases to be of archaeological interest and becomes [the] word of God to contemporary man.[5]

Again I am somewhat puzzled by this treatment of the question. Beasley-Murray asserts that the "human" measures in the text must be "corrected." Then he calls us to a "difficult exercise" by which John's vision becomes the word of God to us. We must ask what is was before it *becomes* the word of God. I grant that the exercise Beasley-Murray calls for is indeed difficult, perhaps even tortuous.

One more example of this approach to the time-frame references is that of Robert H. Mounce.

John writes that these events which constitute the revelation must take place shortly. That more than 1900 years of church history have passed and the end is not yet poses a problem for some. One solution is to understand "shortly" in the sense of suddenly, or without delay once the appointed time arrives. Another approach is to interpret it in terms of the certainty of events in question. Of little help is the suggestion that John may be employing the formula of 2 Peter 3:8 ("with the Lord one day is as a thousand years"). [G. B.] Caird believes that the coming crisis was not the consummation of history but the persecution of the church. Indeed, that did take place shortly. The most satisfying solution is to take the word in a straightforward sense, remembering that in the prophetic outlook the end is always imminent. The perspective is common to the entire New Testament. Jesus taught that God would vindicate his elect without delay (Luke 18:8), and Paul wrote to the Romans that God would soon crush Satan under their feet (Rom. 16:20).[6]

Mounce rejects alternate meanings of *shortly* and opts instead for the word's "straightforward sense." But then he interprets *shortly* in light of the prophetic outlook or perspective that he says is "common to the entire New Testament." The word's "straightforward" meaning is no longer so straightforward. It means something other than its straightforward meaning.

Mounce justifies this with appeals to Jesus and Paul, who use similar language for events that obviously (according to Mounce) did not take place "without delay" or "soon."

This type of literary gymnastics has earned for evangelicals the scorn of critics, who prefer to be even more straightforward and declare that the teaching of Jesus and Paul in these instances is simply wrong. These texts are then added to the multitude of imminent texts in the New Testament to dispute the inspiration and authority of the Bible. Preterists agree that Jesus used imminent language in the parable of the unjust judge and that Paul did as well in Romans 16:20. But preterists hasten to add that Jesus and Paul are referring to events that did take place in the first century, by which the suffering Christians were vindicated and a crushing blow was delivered to Satan.

Preterist interpretation of Revelation follows closely preterist interpretation of the Olivet Discourse. Though preterists differ on *how much* of the Revelation and of the discourse refers to the destruction of Jerusalem, they all regard the main substance of both to refer to the same event: Jesus' coming in judgment on the Jewish nation.

Russell, like other preterists, sees the explicit time-frame references of the Apocalypse as the key to interpreting the book. "It may truly be said that the key has all the while hung by the door, plainly visible to every one who had eyes to see," he writes. "Yet men have tried to pick the lock, or force the door, or climb up some other way, rather than avail themselves of so simple and ready a way of admission as to use the key made and provided for them."[7]

Groups of Time-Frame References

Kenneth L. Gentry Jr., a postmillenarian preterist, refers to the time-frame references in the Apocalypse by listing them according to three basic categories. "The temporal expectation receives frequent repetition in that it occurs not only seven times in the opening and closing chapters, but at least three times in the letters in chapters two and three (Rev. 2:16; 3:11)," Gentry writes. "This expectation is also varied in its manner of expression, almost as if to avoid any potential confusion as to the specificity of its meaning. Its variation revolves among three word groups."[8]

The first word group Gentry treats is that of *taxos*. This term is usually translated either "shortly" or "quickly." It appears in Revelation 1:1; 2:16; 3:11; 22:6, 7, 12, 20. Gentry writes:

> The translation under question (i.e., in Revelation 1:1, although the other references cited should be kept in mind, as well) has to do with the proper interpretation of the Greek phrase *en taxei*. *Taxei* is the dative singular of the noun *taxos*. Lexicographers seem to be universally agreed with the translators as to the meaning of the word. According to the [Bauer,] Arndt and Gingrich *Lexicon*, *taxos* is used in the Septuagint (and certain non-canonical writings) to mean "speed, quickness, swiftness, haste." In the prepositional phrase *en taxei*, the word is used adverbially in the Septuagint and Josephus to mean "quickly, at once, without delay." The New Testament uses *taxos* in this manner, says [Bauer,] Arndt and Gingrich, in Acts 10:33; 12:7; 17:15; 22:18. In Luke 18:8; Romans 16:20; 1 Timothy 3:14; Revelation 1:1; and 22:6, this lexicon translates it "soon, in a short time."[9]

Gentry cites similar entries from Joseph Henry Thayer, G. Abbott-Smith, F. J. A. Hort, and Kurt Aland.[10] Gentry argues that commentators would render the term differently from the lexicographical consensus only if influenced by an interpretive controlling *a priori*.

The second word group is the *engus* group. This term, translated "near" or "at hand," is used in Revelation 1:3 and 22:10. It is a time-frame reference indicating events that are imminent. Gentry argues:

> How could events related to the collapse of the Roman Empire two or three hundred years in the future be considered "at hand," as per [Henry Barclay] Swete, [Albert] Barnes, and others? Several generations of these Christians would have waxed and waned over such a period. Even more difficult to understand is how events two or three *thousand* years in the future could be considered "at

Table 6.1

Time-Frame References in Revelation

Shortly, quickly

1:1	. . . things which must shortly take place.
2:16	Repent, or else I will come to you quickly.
3:11	Behold, I come quickly!
22:6	. . . things which must shortly take place.
22:7	Behold, I am coming quickly!
22:12	Behold, I am coming quickly.
22:20	Surely I am coming quickly.

Near, at hand

| 1:3 | The time is near. |
| 22:10 | The time is at hand. |

About to, on the point of

| 1:19 | Write . . . the things that are about to take place. |
| 3:10 | . . . the hour of trial . . . is about to come upon the whole world. |

hand," as per [Robert H.] Mounce, [John] Walvoord, and others. How could such events so remotely stretched out into the future be "at hand"? But if the expected events were to occur within a period of from one to five years—as in the case with Revelation if the book were written prior to A.D. 70—then all becomes clear.[11]

The third word group is *mellō*, which is found in Revelation 1:19 and 3:10. "Certainly it is true that the verb *mellō* can indicate simply 'destined,' or it can be employed in a weakened sense as a periphrasis for the future tense," Gentry says. "Nevertheless, when used with the aorist infinitive—as in Revelation 1:19—the word's preponderate usage and preferred meaning is: 'be on the point of, be about to.' The same is true when the word is used with the present infinitive, as in Rev. 3:10. The basic meaning in both Thayer and Abbott-Smith is: 'to be about to.'"[12]

This triad of word groups points to the nearness of the things foretold in the Book of Revelation. These time-frame references follow closely those of the Olivet Discourse. The major objection to this position, however, regards the dating of Revelation. If the book was written after A.D. 70, then its contents manifestly do not refer to events surrounding the fall of Jerusalem—unless the book is a wholesale fraud, having been composed after the predicted events had already occurred.

The burden for preterists then is to demonstrate that Revelation was written *before* A.D. 70. This burden became the thesis of Gentry's doctoral dissertation. His book *Before Jerusalem Fell* has been welcomed both by advocates of preterism and by its opponents. Jay E. Adams says of *Before Jerusalem Fell:* "Here is a book some of us have been awaiting for years! Now that it is here we can rejoice. Mr. Gentry convincingly demonstrates the fact the book of Revelation was written, as it in so many ways declares, prior to the destruction of Jerusalem in A.D. 70. It should receive a wide reading and ought to rattle many windows."[13]

George W. Knight, who is not a preterist, says this: "*Before Jerusalem Fell* is a thorough and outstanding statement of the case for the early date of Revelation. The book makes one aware of the evidence from within the book and from early church sources, and surveys the arguments of New Testament scholars of this century and previous centuries concerning the question. No stone is left unturned to resolve the question."[14]

When questions of dating biblical books arise, one must consider two main kinds of evidence: *external* and *internal*. As the word suggests, external evidence looks to material apart from and outside the book itself, such as the testimony of ancient writers or citations, quotes, or allusions from other writers, and so forth. The significance of the external evidence for dating Revelation has often been hotly contested. Scholarly opinion has vacillated through the years. Gentry reports:

Around 1800, dates for the New Testament canon ranged very conservatively between A.D. 50 and A.D. 100. By 1850, due to the Tübingen school of thought and under the special influence of F. C. Baur, the range of dates had widened from A.D. 50+ to A.D. 160+. Regarding Revelation's date under the sway of Tübingen, "it was a striking paradox that the Tübingen School which left Paul with only four or, as put by [Adolf] Hilgenfeld in a more moderate form, with only seven authentic Epistles, and brought most of the New Testament documents down to a late date, should in the case of the Apocalypse have affirmed apostolic authorship and a date [a] quarter of a century earlier than that assigned by tradition."[15]

Though conceding that in twentieth-century scholarly circles the majority have placed the writing of Revelation well after A.D. 70, Gentry lists numerous scholars who place it earlier. This list includes Greg L. Bahnsen, Adam Clarke, F. W. Farrar, John A. T. Robinson, Henry Barclay Swete, Milton S. Terry, Wilhelm Bousset, F. F. Bruce, Rudolf Bultmann, Samuel Davidson, Alfred Edersheim, Johann Eichhorn, Joseph A. Fitzmyer, J. B. Lightfoot, C. F. D. Moule, and Augustus H. Strong, to name but a few.[16]

Two things can be said of this list. First, it represents scholars from every point on the theological spectrum. And second, the list, in itself, does not prove an early-date theory, as the theory cannot be demonstrated by counting noses. The list does reveal, however, that the notion of an early date for Revelation is by no means a novelty.

Irenaeus and Clement

The chief argument for a late date for Revelation rests on external evidence, specifically the testimony of the church father Irenaeus (A.D. 130–202). Irenaeus referred to Revelation in a work he wrote near the end of the second century, probably between A.D. 180 and 190. Irenaeus's credibility is enhanced, not only by his important defense of the faith, but also by his claim to be a personal acquaintance of Polycarp, who in turn had known the Apostle John himself. Irenaeus's testimony regarding Revelation is

Table 6.2

Sources of Information
Concerning John and Revelation

Name	Birth	Death	Place of residence
Apollonius of Tyana	1st century		Greece
Clement		c. 101	Rome
Polycarp	c. 69	155	Smyrna
Papias	2d century		Phrygia
Irenaeus	c. 130	c. 202	Gaul
Clement	c. 150	c. 215	Alexandria
Tertullian	c. 160	c. 230	Carthage
Eusebius	c. 260	c. 339	Caesaria
Epiphanius	c. 315	403	Palestine, Cyprus
Jerome	c. 347	c. 420	Bethlehem
Arethas	c. 860		Caesaria
Theophylact	c. 1050	c. 1109	Ochrida

found in book 5 of his famous work *Against Heresies.* This work
has not been preserved in Greek, surviving only in Latin translation. Eusebius cited Irenaeus's comments on Revelation, however, and Gentry provides a detailed analysis of this Greek text.
This has been rendered in English as follows: "We will not, however, incur the risk of pronouncing positively as to the name of
Antichrist; for if it were necessary that his name should be dis-
tinctly revealed in this present time, it would have been
announced by him who beheld the apocalyptic vision. For that
was seen no very long time since, but almost in our day, towards
the end of Domitian's reign."[17]

Is the antecedent of *that* (in the final sentence) the vision, or is it John, the one who saw the vision? Is Irenaeus saying that John's *vision* took place during the reign of Domitian (which would date the Book of Revelation after the destruction of Jerusalem)? Or is Iranaeus saying simply that John, who lived into the reign of Domitian, was seen at that late time?

Gentry opts for the latter alternative. He cites the argument of F. H. Chase:

> The logic of the sentences seems to me to require this interpretation. The statement that the vision was seen at the close of Domitian's reign supplies no reason why the mysterious number should have been expounded "by him who saw the apocalypse," had he judged such an exposition needful. If, on the other hand, we refer *heōrathē* to St. John, the meaning is plain and simple. We may expand the sentences thus: "Had it been needful that the explanation of the name should be proclaimed to the men of our own day, that explanation would have been given by the author of the Book. For the author was seen on earth, he lived and held converse with his disciples, not so very long ago, but almost in our own generation. Thus, on the one hand, he lived years after he wrote the Book, and there was abundant opportunity for him to expound the riddle, had he wished to do so; and, on the other hand, since he lived on almost into our generation, the explanation, had he given it, must have been preserved to us."[18]

Though supported by other interpreters of Irenaeus, such as Jacobus Wettstein and James M. Macdonald,[19] Chase's view is speculative. He does not demonstrate conclusively that this is what Irenaeus *had* to mean. Chase merely indicates what Irenaeus *could* have meant, or at best what Irenaeus *probably* meant. Chase does make clear, however, that the words of Irenaeus contain a certain ambiguity. This precludes them from being used as definitive proof for dating the Apocalypse during the reign of Domitian.

Irenaeus also refers to the "ancient copies" of Revelation. This designation is difficult to square with the idea of the original autographs having been composed (according to Irenaeus) "almost in our own generation."

Other important external evidence includes the testimony of Clement of Alexandria (A.D. 150–215). "When after the death of the tyrant," says Clement, "[John the apostle] removed from the island of Patmos to Ephesus, he used to journey by request to the neighbouring districts of the Gentiles, in some places to appoint bishops, in others to regulate whole churches, in others to set among the clergy some one man, it may be, of those indicated by the Spirit."[20]

Who is "the tyrant?" Clement does not name him. Gentry amasses evidence to support the thesis that the tyrant is not Domitian but Nero. Nero was regarded as the quintessential tyrant and was commonly known by the name *Tyrant*. Gentry cites the testimony of Apollonius of Tyana. "In my travels, which have been wider than ever man yet accomplished, I have seen many, many wild beasts of Arabia and India," writes Apollonius. "But this beast, that is commonly called a Tyrant, I know not how many heads it has, nor if it be crooked of claw, and armed with horrible fangs. . . . And of wild beasts you cannot say that they were ever known to eat their own mothers, but Nero has gorged himself on this diet."[21]

Two other statements by Clement also lend support for the early dating of Revelation. The first is a reference to John pursuing a young apostate on horseback during the period *after* John's exile. If he was exiled during the reign of Domitian, then John would have been in his nineties when chasing the apostate. While not impossible, such a feat is not likely.

The second statement comes from Clement's *Miscellanies:* "For the teaching of our Lord at His advent, beginning with Augustus and Tiberius, was completed in the middle of the times of Tiberius. And that of the apostles, embracing the ministry of Paul, *ends with Nero.*"[22]

Since Clement considered the Apostle John the author of Revelation and Clement argues that apostolic revelation ceased with Nero, Clement therefore believes that Revelation was written before Nero died.

After canvassing other external sources from antiquity, Gentry provides the following summary: "There are some witnesses that may hint at a pre-A.D. 70 dating for Revelation, such as *The*

Shepherd of Hermas and Papias. Yet, other sources are even more suggestive of a Neronic banishment: the Muratorian Canon, Tertullian, and Epiphanius. Others seem to imply *both* dates for John's banishment: Eusebius (cf. *Ecclesiastical History* with *Evangelical Demonstrations*) and Jerome. . . . On the other hand, undeniably supportive of a Neronic date are Arethas, the Syriac *History of John*, the Syriac versions of Revelation, and Theophylact."[23]

Gentry recognizes that the external evidence regarding the dating of Revelation is neither monolithic nor homogeneous, but he argues that the preponderance of this evidence supports a Neronic date.

The internal evidence for an early date of Revelation involves the content of the Apocalypse itself, as well as the life situation reflected in its pages. J. Stuart Russell sees Revelation as the Apostle John's extended version of the Olivet Discourse. Gentry declares that the central theme of Revelation is the coming destruction of Jerusalem and the end of the Jewish dispensation. In addition to the time-frame references already considered, he makes his case by analyzing several motifs.

The Identity of the Sixth King

Reference to the sixth king is found in chapter 17:

But the angel said to me, "Why did you marvel? I will tell you the mystery of the woman and of the beast that carries her, which has the seven heads and the ten horns. The beast that you saw was, and is not, and will ascend out of the bottomless pit and go to perdition. And those who dwell on the earth will marvel, whose names are not written in the Book of Life from the foundation of the world, when they see the beast that was, and is not, and yet is. Here is the mind which has wisdom: The seven heads are seven mountains on which the woman sits. There are also seven kings. Five have fallen, one is, and the other has not yet come. And when he comes, he must continue a short time. And the beast that was, and is not, is himself also the eighth, and is of the seven, and is going to perdition. And the ten horns which you saw are ten kings

who have received no kingdom as yet, but they receive authority
for one hour as kings with the beast."

(Rev. 17:7–17)

Who is the sixth king? In the quest to identify him, one encounters two problems: (1) Does the term *king* refer to a Roman emperor? (2) What is the proper way to count these emperors? Gentry and others link the reference to seven hills with Rome, which was known as the "City of Seven Hills." If this linkage is correct, then it would seem that the king is a Roman ruler.

Revelation specifically mentions seven kings. Five are said to have fallen. One is referred to in the present tense. The seventh has not yet come, and when he does he will not remain for long. Charles Cutler Torrey says of this reference that "this certainly seems to provide, as exactly as could be expected of an apocalypse, information as to the time—the precise reign—in which the book was composed."[24]

Though Julius Caesar preferred the title caesar to king, it was common in the ancient world to refer to Rome's emperors, including Julius, as kings. Even the New Testament bears witness to this when the chief priests declare to Pontius Pilate, "We have no king but Caesar" (John 19:15).

We are still left with the question of the proper method of counting the Roman rulers. Augustus was the first to refer to himself as emperor. Since he followed Julius Caesar, do we begin counting with Julius or Augustus? Basically two different approaches have been made to the question. One approach is to start with Augustus, as in table 6.3, option 1. In this list the sixth king is Galba, whose reign was brief. Those who use this approach, however, frequently skip over Galba, Otho, and Vitellius, since they were in power only briefly during the struggle for supremacy that followed the death of Nero. If they are omitted from the list (see table 6.3, option 2), then the sixth king is Vespasian, during whose reign Jerusalem was destroyed. If the sixth king is Vespasian, then we still fall short of the reign of Domitian, which is the time-frame usually given for the late date of Revelation.

Table 6.3

The Sixth King of Revelation 17:10

Option 1	Option 2	Option 3	Reign
		1. Julius Caesar	49–44
1. Augustus	1. Augustus	2. Augustus	31–14
2. Tiberius	2. Tiberius	3. Tiberius	14–37
3. Caligula	3. Caligula	4. Caligula	37–41
4. Claudius	4. Claudius	5. Claudius	41–54
5. Nero	5. Nero	**6. Nero**	54–68
6. Galba			68–69
7. Otho			69–69
8. Vitellius			69–69
9. Vespasian	**6. Vespasian**		69–79

A more natural approach, however, is to begin the list of kings with Julius Caesar, as was the custom of ancient historians such as Josephus and Suetonius, as well as Dio Cassius. In this series (see table 6.3, option 3), the sixth king is Nero. If he is the king referred to in Revelation in the present tense, then this adds considerable weight to the argument for dating the book in the mid- to late-sixties.

The Presence of the Temple

If the Book of Revelation was written after the destruction of Jerusalem and the temple, it seems strange that John would be silent about these cataclysmic events. Granted this is an argument from silence, but the silence is deafening. Not only does

Fig. 6.1

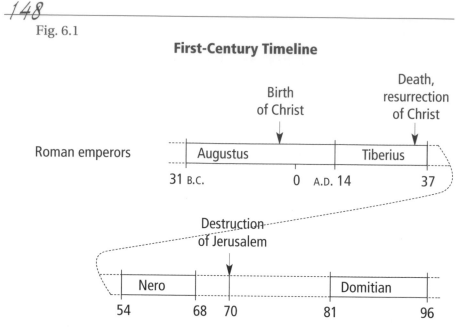

First-Century Timeline

Revelation not mention the temple's destruction as a past event, it frequently refers to the temple as still standing. This is seen clearly in Revelation 11. "The time of the Apocalypse is also definitely fixed," writes Bernhard Weiss (cited by Gentry), "by the fact that according to the prophecy in chap. 11 it was manifestly written before the destruction of Jerusalem, which in 11:1 is only anticipated."[25]

Arguments against Weiss's thesis are based largely on the writings of Clement of Rome. Tradition has it that Clement wrote during the last decade of the first century. Donald Guthrie and Robert H. Mounce, for example, argue that Clement spoke of the temple as still standing and of sacrifices still being made in Jerusalem.[26] Some contend that Clement was speaking in the "ideal present," others that he was referring to on-going sacrifices by a Jewish remnant near the temple site. But if Clement is actually declaring that the temple still stands in Jerusalem, then we must conclude one of the following: (1) He was wrong; (2) Jerusalem was not destroyed until at least twenty years after A.D. 70; or (3) Clement wrote before Jerusalem was destroyed.

The least credible option is the second. The A.D. 70 date is one of the best attested in all of ancient history. The first option is also highly unlikely. Surely Clement was aware of the temple's destruction if he wrote in the nineties. Unless we assume that he was speaking in some idealized sense, the most likely option is the third: that he wrote his letter *before* Jerusalem fell. Gentry gives impressive evidence to support this conclusion.

Gentry canvasses other internal evidence for an early date of Revelation, such as the question of emperor worship, the role of Jewish Christianity, the looming Jewish war, and the role of Nero (to which we will devote more attention later.) "My confident conviction," concludes Gentry, "is that a solid case for a Neronic date for Revelation can be set forth from the available evidences, both internal and external. In fact, I would lean toward a date after the outbreak of the Neronic persecution in late A.D. 64 and before the declaration of the Jewish War in early A.D. 67. A date in either A.D. 65 or early A.D. 66 would seem most suitable. My hope is that the debate will be renewed with vigor and care, for the matter is more than a merely academic or intellectual exercise; it has ramifications in the area of practical Christianity."[27]

*The Lord Himself will descend
from heaven with a shout,
with the voice of an archangel,
and with the trumpet of God.*

(1 Thess. 4:16)

7

When Is the Resurrection?

The resurgence of preterism in our day has appeared in various forms and degrees. It is anything but monolithic in its viewpoint, and it has engendered debate, at times sharp, among its advocates.

The different schools of preterism have been described in various ways. Kenneth L. Gentry Jr., for example, distinguishes his position from that of J. Stuart Russell, Max R. King, and others by calling his own position (as well as that of Gary DeMar, the early David Chilton, and others) *orthodox preterism*. He refers to the position advocated by the others with a variety of terms including *hyper-preterism, consistent preterism,* and *full preterism.* I have sought to distinguish the two camps by using such terms as *radical preterism* and *moderate preterism.*

As the debate has unfolded, the labels themselves have generated no small degree of disagreement. Edward E. Stevens has responded to Gentry's essay "A Brief Theological Analysis of Hyper-Preterism" with a booklet entitled simply *Stevens' Response to Gentry.*[1] These two essays put the differences between the two schools in bold relief. Stevens takes umbrage at Gentry's use of the term *hyper-preterism*. He winces at the pejorative connotation of the prefix *hyper-*, which often suggests an extremist or unbalanced viewpoint.

The term *radical* suffers from the same fate. When I use the term, I mean "that which holds something as a core belief." The term *radical* comes from the Latin *radix*, which means "root." But terms tend to take on nuances, and in our culture the word *radical* conjures up more than I wish to impose on any school of preterism. So it is probably better that I now modify my own descriptive language.

Before embarking on his critique, Gentry makes this observation: ". . . there are numerous exegetical and theological problems I have with the hyper-preterist viewpoint. I deem my historic, orthodox preterism to be exegetical preterism (because I find specific passages calling for specific preterist events); I deem Max King and Ed Stevens' views to be theological preterism or comprehensive preterism (they apply exegetical conclusions drawn from several eschatological passages to all eschatological passages because of their theological paradigm.)"[2]

Gentry distinguishes between "exegetical preterism" and "theological preterism." This distinction is not all that helpful. Gentry's view is intensely theological, and that of Stevens and others is vitally concerned with exegesis. Gentry is charging that comprehensive preterists are driven to their "consistent" viewpoint by their theological paradigm.

Stevens responds to Gentry:

> It's not clear what Gentry intended to communicate when he used the term "hyper" in "hyper-preterist." Surely he is not using it for ridicule or derisive purposes, although others on the Internet have so used it. I fail to see what point Gentry is making, that could not be made with a less pejorative term. Why not simply stick with "consistent preterist" (as in his opening paragraph), or "comprehensive preterist" (as in his third paragraph)? Actually the term "preterist" is all that is needed to describe our view. "Preterist" means past in fulfillment. Only those who take a past fulfillment

of all the eschatological events (e.g. the return of Christ, resurrection, judgment) can rightly be called "preterist." Those who believe the major eschatological events (i.e. Second Coming, Resurrection, Judgment) are still future are really just another kind of futurist. So Gentry and

Two Kinds of Preterism	
Full Preterism	**Partial Preterism**
Consistent preterism	
Radical preterism	Moderate preterism
Theological preterism	Exegetical preterism
Hyper-preterism	Orthodox preterism

other "partial Preterists" should more properly be labeled amil or postmillennial historicists or futurists. Only someone who puts all of the eschatological events in the past can rightly be called "preterist" in the true sense of the term. . . . The term "preterist" belongs to the "full preterist," not to the "partial preterist" futurists like Gentry.[3]

This debate over labels may seem like a tempest in a teapot. It brings to mind the controversy John Calvin had concerning the term *substance*. Calvin had to wage war on two fronts, debating both with those who argued for the presence of the "substance" of Christ's body in the sacrament and with the spiritualists who denied the presence of Christ in the sacrament altogether. When arguing with the former, he avoided the term *substance* because it conveyed the idea of corporal or physical substance. When arguing with the latter, he insisted that *substance* means, not the physical presence, but the "real" presence of Christ in the sacrament.

This illustrates that the parties in a dispute often use language in different ways. Like Calvin, Gentry has been debating on two fronts. On the one side he is engaging Dispensationalism with its futurism. Against them he argues for a limited preterism with reference to specific prophecies that he believes were fulfilled in A.D. 70. On the other side he is engaging full preterists. Against them Gentry stresses events that he believes have not yet been fulfilled.

Though Stevens prefers that the term *preterist* be reserved for those who believe that all eschatological events have been fulfilled in the past, he nevertheless refers to Gentry as a "partial preterist." Maybe the terms that best describe the two positions are *full preterism* and *partial preterism*. Both are preterist with respect to *some* eschatological events, but both are not preterist with respect to *all* eschatological events. The terms *full* and *partial* can then be safely applied to these two positions.

Preterism and the Creeds

Gentry criticizes full preterism sharply, arguing that it falls outside the scope of orthodox Christianity. At least from a creedal perspective, Gentry says it is heterodoxy (or heresy). "No creed allows any second Advent in A.D. 70," he writes. "No creed allows any other type of resurrection than a bodily one. Historic creeds speak of the universal, personal judgment of all men, not of a representative judgment in A.D. 70. It would be most remarkable if the entire church that came through A.D. 70 missed the proper understanding of the eschaton and did not realize its members had been resurrected!"[4]

Before exploring Stevens's response to the charge of heterodoxy, we must note in passing that Gentry succinctly summarizes the theological issues involved: a future parousia, a future judgment, and a future resurrection. These are crucial eschatological events that partial preterists say have not yet been fulfilled. Surely Gentry is correct when asserting that the historic creeds of Christendom are virtually unanimous in regarding these events as future.

Stevens defends full preterism from the charge of heresy, not by arguing that the creeds in fact support this position, but by arguing that the creeds are not the final test of orthodoxy. The ultimate test is conformity to Scripture, not to the creeds. He points out that the Reformed tradition is adamant about this. The Reformation principle of *sola Scriptura* was forged in this crucible. "Full Preterists are Reformers," Stevens says, "and as such it should be obvious that we believe the early church and the creeds can be (and have been found to be) mistaken."[5]

Obviously the full preterists have no desire to deviate from Scripture. They bear the burden in this controversy of showing

Table 7.1

Differences between Preterists

	Full Preterists		Partial Preterists	
	A.D. 70	*At the end of history*	*A.D. 70*	*At the end of history*
Coming (parousia) of Christ	yes	no	yes	yes
Resurrection and rapture	yes	no	no	yes
Day of the Lord	yes	no	yes	yes
Judgment	yes	no	yes	yes

that creedal orthodoxy has been wrong at crucial points of eschatological understanding. This is a weighty burden, an enormous onus of responsibility. I do not believe that Gentry has a slavish view of the creeds or that he thinks any or all of them have the authority of Scripture. Gentry is fully committed to the Reformation principle of *sola Scriptura.* But strong advocates of *sola Scriptura* historically have had great respect for the historic creeds. These advocates have not considered the creeds infallible, but they have held the creeds in extremely high esteem.

Personally I cringe at the idea of going against such a unified and strong testimony to the historic faith, even though I grant the possibility that they are wrong at points. All who are inclined to differ with the creeds should observe a warning light and show great caution. Of course this warning light pales in comparison to the authority of Scripture itself.

I was somewhat taken aback while reading Stevens on this point when he included in his argument a quote from my own lips. "If we don't take a full preterist approach," Stevens writes, "we leave the integrity of Jesus and the New Testament writers utterly defenseless. *Certainly, it impugns the interpretative accuracy of the historic church in matters of eschatology, but as R. C. Sproul observed, '. . . people have attacked the credibility of Jesus. Maybe some Church Fathers made a mistake. Maybe our favorite theologians have made mistakes. I can abide with that. I can't abide with Jesus' being a false prophet.'* [We need to state it clearly for the record that R. C. Sproul, Sr. is not a full preterist, but he does see a lot of merit in the partial preterist approach similar to Ken Gentry.]"[6]

It is comforting to be quoted accurately. I did say what Stevens says I said. I agree with all preterists that what is at stake here is the authority of Jesus, and we must be consumed with maintaining his authority. To be completely candid, I must confess that I am still unsettled on some crucial matters. I am convinced that the substance of the Olivet Discourse was fulfilled in A.D. 70 and that the bulk of Revelation was likewise fulfilled in that time-frame. I share Gentry's concerns about full preterism, particularly on such issues as the consummation of the kingdom and the resurrection of the dead. In the final analysis I am confident that both Stevens and Gentry agree that these matters must be settled on the basis of biblical exegesis. Let us turn our attention then to the biblical questions that remain unresolved between partial and full preterists.

The central issue is this: What events prophesied in the Bible are as yet unfulfilled. Full preterists refer to themselves as "consistent" preterists, implying that partial preterists are "inconsistent." Full preterists apply a strict view of the meaning of *parousia, end of the age,* and *the day of the Lord.*

While partial preterists acknowledge that in the destruction of Jerusalem in A.D. 70 there was *a* parousia or coming of Christ, they maintain that it was not *the* parousia. That is, the coming of Christ in A.D. 70 was a coming in judgment on the Jewish nation, indicating the end of the Jewish age and the fulfillment of a day of the Lord. Jesus really did come in judgment at this time, fulfilling his prophecy in the Olivet Discourse. But this was not the final or ultimate coming of Christ. The parousia, in its fullness, will extend far beyond the Jewish nation and will be universal in its scope and significance. It will come, not at the end of the Jewish age, but at the end of human history as we know it. It will be, not merely a day of the Lord, but the final and ultimate day of the Lord.

Partial preterists understand that there are nuances to biblical terminology regarding the coming of Christ and the day of the Lord, nuances that make it possible and necessary to speak of more than one event that encompasses all these things at once.

Full preterists, on the other hand, argue that this approach is inconsistent and arbitrary, resulting in multiple comings of Christ and days of the Lord. They insist that time-frame references in the Olivet Discourse supply the supreme key to New Testament prophecy and that this key applies to all references to eschatological events. Stevens objects to Gentry's charge that, according to consistent preterists, "all prophecy is fulfilled in the A.D. 70 destruction of the Temple, including the Second Advent, the resurrection of the dead, the great Judgment, and so forth."[7]

Stevens says this is not "exactly correct" because full preterists believe in an ongoing fulfillment of prophecy in the present kingdom of God. This ongoing fulfillment, however, does not include *specific events* predicted in the New Testament. This seems to be a bit of a quibble. Gentry is clearly speaking about the fulfillment of certain predicted events. What can easily get lost in the quibble is the clear position taken by full preterists: the specific eschatological events predicted in the New Testament, such as the second advent, the resurrection of the dead, the rapture, and the last judgment, have already taken place.

This position is greeted by partial preterists with the charge of heresy and heterodoxy. Full preterists agree that their views depart from *creedal* orthodoxy, but insist they do not depart from *biblical* orthodoxy. Both sides agree that in the final analysis the test for orthodoxy must be the Bible, not the creeds.

One point of creedal orthodoxy is the Apostle's Creed's affirmation of the resurrection of the body *(resurrectionis carnis)*. This affirmation refers to the resurrection not of Christ's body (which is affirmed earlier in the creed), but of our bodies. It declares that Christians will participate in the bodily resurrection of Christ when our bodies are raised and glorified on the last day. This view is categorically rejected by full preterists and constitutes a major difference between the two views.

The Resurrection of the Body

The chief text focusing on the resurrection of the body is found in 1 Corinthians 15.

> Now this I say, brethren, that flesh and blood cannot inherit the kingdom of God; nor does corruption inherit incorruption. Behold, I tell you a mystery: We shall not all sleep, but we shall all be changed—in a moment, in the twinkling of an eye, at the last trumpet. For the trumpet will sound, and the dead will be raised incorruptible, and we shall be changed. For this corruptible must put on incorruption, and this mortal must put on immortality. So when this corruptible has put on incorruption, and this mortal has put on immortality, then shall be brought to pass the saying that is written: "Death is swallowed up in victory."
>
> "O Death, where is your sting?
> O Hades, where is your victory?"
>
> The sting of death is sin, and the strength of sin is the law. But thanks be to God, who gives us the victory through our Lord Jesus Christ. Therefore, my beloved brethren, be steadfast, immovable, always abounding in the work of the Lord, knowing that your labor is not in vain in the Lord.
>
> *(1 Cor. 15:50–58)*

Full preterists make two strong assertions about this text: It refers to a *spiritual* resurrection, not a *bodily* resurrection; and this resurrection has already taken place. Again the time-frame is crucial to the discussion. Russell stresses the apostle's words in verse 51: "We shall not all sleep, but we shall all be changed. . . ." "To whom does the apostle refer when he says, '*We* shall not all sleep,' etc.?" Russell asks. "Is it to some hypothetical persons living in some distant age of time, or is it of the Corinthians and himself that he is thinking? Why should he think of the distant future when it is certain that he considered the Parousia to be imminent?"[8]

According to Russell most of those who received Paul's Letter to the Corinthians could have lived, and would have expected to live, long enough to see the events Paul described. To maintain that these events were indeed fulfilled in the first century, one must interpret the relevant passages in a way that makes early fulfillment possible. The most severe obstacle is the absence of any historical record that the rapture of the living and the resurrection of the dead occurred. So Russell and other full preterists conceive of the resurrection of the dead in spiritual terms. Russell anticipates this objection:

> But the objection will recur, How could all this take place without notice or record? First, as regards the resurrection of the dead, it is to be considered how little we know of its conditions and characteristics. Must it come with observation? Must it be cognizable by material organs? "It is raised a spiritual body." Is a spiritual body one which can be seen, touched, handled? We are not certain that the eye can see the spiritual, or the hand grasp the immaterial. On the contrary, the presumption and the probability are that they cannot. All this resurrection of the dead and transmutation of the living take place in the region of the spiritual, into which earthly spectators and reporters do not enter, and could see nothing if they did.[9]

Here we see a marked change in Russell's exegetical approach from the one he applied to the time-frame references in the Olivet Discourse. In the Olivet Discourse the interpreter faces the problem of dealing with both time-frame references and references to the parousia. As we have seen, some commentators "spiritualize" the time-frame language and see it as being somewhat figurative, while interpreting images that describe the parousia more literally. Russell treats the time-frame references literally and the parousia images figuratively. In this respect he has the precedent of Old Testament–judgment prophecy on his side.

When we get to the Corinthian correspondence, we notice two things immediately. The first is that the time-frame adopted by Russell is based not on an explicit chronological reference, but on an inference drawn from Paul's words "we shall not all sleep."

If we conclude that Paul, by divine inspiration, is predicting that the resurrection will occur while he is still alive, then the resurrection occurred at least five years prior to the destruction of Jerusalem (Paul was martyred under Nero in A.D. 65).

The full preterist might argue that the "we" does not include Paul himself, but simply some who received his teaching. But if this is the case, then it is likewise possible that the "we who are alive" can be even more inclusive and refers to any reader of the Corinthian text in the future.

The "we" passage of 1 Corinthians is far less specific concerning the time of the resurrection than are Jesus' words in the Olivet Discourse. The more serious problem, however, is the full preterists' treatment of the *character* of the resurrection. They view the resurrection as a hidden, "spiritual" resurrection, and they must view it this way for full preterism to work.

We encounter two more-serious problems with this view. The first is logical, the second theological. The logical difficulty is that it involves propositions and assertions that can be neither verified nor falsified empirically. To be sure, purely rational arguments that rest solely on deduction do not require empirical verification. But if one announces or predicts things that will take place in the arena of real history involving physical reality, then empirical verification becomes relevant and crucial.

Russell labors the point that a spiritual body need not be resurrected under the conditions of empirical observation. He asks if a spiritual body can be seen, touched, or handled? Paul's use of the term *spiritual body* is what gives license to this type of speculation. It is unfortunate that the apostle failed to alert the Corinthians—and us, by extension—that he was speaking of a secret, hidden, spiritual resurrection. His language certainly suggests something else, particularly as Paul so clearly conjoins the resurrection of our bodies with the resurrection of Christ's body. The resurrected Christ is the firstfruits of all who will be raised. The apostle clearly teaches that our resurrections will be patterned after the resurrection of Christ:

> But now Christ is risen from the dead, and has become the firstfruits of those who have fallen asleep. For since by man came

death, by Man also came the resurrection of the dead. For as in Adam all die, even so in Christ all shall be made alive. But each one in his own order: Christ the firstfruits, afterward those who are Christ's at His coming. Then comes the end, when He delivers the kingdom to God the Father, when He puts an end to all rule and all authority and power. For He must reign till He has put all enemies under His feet. The last enemy that will be destroyed is death.

(1 Cor. 15:20–26)

The New Testament accounts of Christ's resurrection reveal that in his resurrected body there is both continuity and discontinuity. Obviously his body underwent some sort of change. It became a glorified human body. To the extent that this glorification involved change in his physical composition we can speak of discontinuity. But the Bible lays great stress on the continuity of the body that was placed in the tomb with the body that was raised. It was not *a* body. It was the *same* body.

My human body has not been glorified. It undergoes certain biological and chemical changes every moment. It is constantly and relentlessly aging. But though my body is never totally the same from moment to moment, it is nevertheless substantially the same. The body I had yesterday was not annihilated and replaced with an utterly new body today. Despite the changes taking place in my body at the moment, there remains a real continuity with my former body. My present body contains teeth that I have had for decades and scars that have blemished my skin since childhood.

When we assert of Jesus that the same body that died on the cross and was buried in the tomb was then resurrected, we acknowledge that his body underwent certain changes. But it is crucial that after the resurrection, the tomb was empty. Today the graves of the saints who have died since the destruction of Jerusalem are not empty. If these bodies had been resurrected, there would be a radical discontinuity between them and the bodies that had been buried. Indeed the discontinuity would be so profound that it would probably be more accurate to say that they had been "reincarnated" rather than resurrected, or that resurrection is such a spiritual thing that neither the body nor physical matter of any type has anything to do with it.

Invisible and Untouchable?

Russell says that perhaps our spiritual bodies may not be seen, touched, or handled. If that is the case, then not only is there radical discontinuity between our earthly bodies and our heavenly bodies, but also there is a radical discontinuity between the nature of our resurrected bodies and the nature of Christ's. In his resurrected state Christ was seen, touched, and handled.

Again to argue that the resurrection applies exclusively to the realm of the spiritual is to make it nonverifiable and nonfalsifiable. This is dangerous business. It smacks of the type of argument one hears on behalf of poltergeists. Some argue that poltergeists are allergic to scientists and always disappear when one comes near. Some argue that little green men on the moon have a built-in antipathy to telescopes. The existence of such things can never be falsified because the terms of falsification are limited at the outset.

This is not to say that Russell is arguing in identical form to those who avow the existence of poltergeists or little green men. Russell is trying to deal seriously with Scripture, which he believed is the infallible Word of God. My point, however, is that his arguments concerning resurrection are fraught with peril and beg the question.

For Russell's arguments to work they must be squeezed into a framework that also raises serious theological questions. As we have already indicated, his arguments raise questions concerning the nature, not only of *our* resurrected bodies, but also of Christ's resurrected body. If a spiritual body cannot be seen, touched, or handled, is it a body at all? It is one thing to say that our resurrected bodies will be *spiritual* bodies, but quite another to imply that our resurrected bodies will be merely *spirits*. The Bible speaks of spiritual *bodies*. Though the body will undergo changes during its glorification, it will still be a body.

Russell concludes his analysis of 1 Corinthians 15 by reducing the problem of interpretation to the following dilemma: (1) Either Paul was guided by the Spirit of God and the events Paul predicted came to pass, or (2) the apostle was mistaken and these events did not take place. We agree that if the problem is stated in this manner, option 1 is preferable. Russell's conclusion, however, strongly implies the fallacy of the false dilemma, also called the "either/or" fallacy. This means that the options are reduced to two when there may be more alternatives.

Russell implies in the context that Paul could have been speaking the truth only if he was speaking of a spiritual resurrection. This approach is driven by Russell's conviction that all eschatological events predicted in the New Testament fall within the framework of the destruction of Jerusalem. He assumes that the only meaning for "the end" is the end of the Jewish age and that nothing is predicted for the end of the world. He views the judgment of God on Israel as the last and final judgment.

In our day Max R. King has written voluminously in support of full preterism and a spiritual resurrection. He argues that there are three successive stages in the resurrection of the dead. He sets these forth as follows:

Concerning stage 1, the resurrection of Christ marked the beginning of the resurrection of the dead. He was the firstfruits of them that slept (1 Cor. 15:20). His Messianic (age-ending) reign began *after* His resurrection because His kingdom was not "of this world"; i.e., not of the Old Covenant aeon (John 18:36).

Concerning stage 2, the death and resurrection of the pre–end-of-the-age saints covers the time of Christ's pre-parousia reign from the cross to the A.D. 70 end of the age. It is the completion of the *first resurrection.* The firstfruits die and rise *with Christ* in the sense of dying to the old aeon and rising to the new, hence they live and reign *with Him* in that eschatological period which answers to the symbolic "thousand year reign." They reign *with* Christ (Rev. 20[:4–5]).

Concerning stage 3, the universal resurrection is conjoined with the ultimate establishment of God's universal reign at "the end." This end is the same end as Matt. 24:3, 14—the end of the Jewish age. This was the focal point of the ultimate coming of the king-dom of God in Daniel 7, the Olivet Discourse of Christ (Luke 21:31), and the post-Pentecost apostolic writings (Acts 14:22; Heb. 12:28; 2 Peter 1:11; Rev. 11:15). It was all achieved from the beginning of Christ's reign to the consummated coming of God's kingdom, within the end-time period of Christ's eschatological sayings (Matt. 24:34; Mark 9:1; Matt. 16:27, 28).[10]

This schema indicates a single resurrection that takes place in three distinct stages during one eschatological period. For this schema to work, the traditional idea of resurrection must be replaced with a metaphorical idea of resurrection, dying to an old redemptive age or eon and "rising" to the new eon. This end of the age is the only "end" with which biblical eschatology is con-cerned.

"We contend, therefore," King declares, "that God's consum-mation of historical Israel through Christ marked the end of his-tory. . . . We suggest that the problem lies in the failure of schol-ars to identify the history that is involved in biblical eschatology. Biblical history does have meaning. Its goal has been reached in Christ. The end foreseen by the prophets has come. Death has been destroyed 'in the mountain of the Lord.' The perfect reign of God through Christ has been established in 'the age to come.'"[11]

We notice a kind of equivocation here in King's use of the term *end*. On the one hand it means "the completion of a chronolog-ical time period." On the other it means "aim" or "goal." The two concepts are not inherently incompatible, because a temporal end may indeed coincide with a particular historical goal. This distinction is crucial to King's view, enabling him to say that the consummation of historical Israel "marked the end of history."

This is a strange assertion. King obviously does not mean that the broader moving of world history ceased in A.D. 70. He must mean that the redemptive history of Israel "ended," that it had reached its goal.

Edward E. Stevens indicates that the full-preterist view of the resurrection is not monolithic. He says:

Within the full preterist community there are at least three different views regarding the implications of the resurrection event for
the individual Christian. That may sound like a lot of confusion
among preterists, until you look at the legion of views among futurists. Max King has suggested an approach which focuses almost
exclusively on the collective body of the church being raised out
of the Old Testament Jewish system. This view has some difficulty
explaining the continuity of our resurrection bodies with Christ's
resurrection body, and it forces the exclusive collective body concept into passages which may be dealing with the individual implications of the resurrection instead. J. S. Russell and Milton S. Terry
have suggested a resurrection (in the unseen realm) and a literal
(but unnoticed) rapture at A.D. 70 (the "change") for which (so far)
no historical evidence has surfaced. Others have proposed a resurrection of the dead in the heavenly realm with visible signs being
given in the physical realm, and say that the rapture is just another
description of the invisible "gathering" into the presence of God
at A.D. 70. I would tend to favor this latter view, although Russell
and Terry's idea cannot be lightly dismissed.[12]

Stevens bristles against Gentry's charge that full preterism slips
into a kind of gnosticism with respect to the resurrection. Stevens
cites the work of Murray J. Harris[13] to steer a course between a
totally spiritualized view of the resurrection and a view of full
bodily resurrection. It seems to me that Stevens and other full
preterists he cites go more in the direction of gnosticism than
Harris does.

The Rapture of the Living

The debate over the nature and time of the resurrection is
closely linked with Paul's teaching regarding the rapture. Paul
sets this forth in his First Epistle to the Thessalonians:

But I do not want you to be ignorant, brethren, concerning those
who have fallen asleep, lest you sorrow as others who have no
hope. For if we believe that Jesus died and rose again, even so God

will bring with Him those who sleep in Jesus. For this we say to you by the word of the Lord, that we who are alive and remain until the coming of the Lord will by no means precede those who are asleep. For the Lord Himself will descend from heaven with a shout, with the voice of an archangel, and with the trumpet of God. And the dead in Christ will rise first. Then we who are alive and remain shall be caught up together with them in the clouds to meet the Lord in the air. And thus we shall always be with the Lord. Therefore comfort one another with these words.

(1 Thess. 4:13–18)

Russell treats this text regarding the rapture in much the same way he treats Paul's teaching on resurrection in 1 Corinthians 15. Russell argues that the phrase "we who are alive" (1 Thess. 4:17) indicates that the apostle expected the rapture to occur in his own lifetime. Russell links the rapture with the coming of Christ in judgment on Jerusalem: "It may be said that we have no evidence of such facts having occurred as are here described—the Lord descending with a shout, the sounding of the trumpet, the raising of the sleeping dead, the rapture of the living saints. True, but is it certain that these are facts cognisable by the senses? Is their place in the region of the material and the visible?"[14]

To maintain a past fulfillment of the rapture, Russell argues for a "secret" rapture that takes place in the non-physical, spiritual realm. He admits there is no evidence that these events occurred as described. But this is because the events described took place in the non-sensory realm.

If this is the case, why did the apostle use the language he did? He said the Lord would descend with a shout, but Russell says nobody could hear it. The voice of the archangel is silent, and the trumpet of God is mute. Not only this, but the multitude of the rising dead were caught up invisibly into invisible clouds to meet the invisible, coming Lord.

This raises severe questions of hermeneutics. One can legitimately take the descriptive language of the Olivet Discourse in a figurative way, because the language is so similar to Old Testament prophetic imagery. But Paul's language in 1 Thessalonians

4 is clearly of a different sort. Here the genre of the text makes it highly unlikely that Paul was describing an event hidden from earthly view.

Max R. King argues that the language of the rapture, like that of the Olivet Discourse, is *apocalyptic imagery.* "In these and other related passages dealing with the End, or the Day of the Lord, the sounding of the trumpet is not to be understood in a literal sense," King writes. "The language is symbolic, calling attention to the eschatological action of God in the consummation of the age. Being caught up together in the clouds to meet the Lord in the air simply is accommodative language denoting the end-of-the-age gathering together of God's elect (Eph. 1:10)."[15] King links the trumpet image with that used in the Olivet Discourse in Matthew 24:31. In both loci he sees it as the symbol of a spiritual truth.

Others have argued that the description of the rapture adapts a Roman ceremony of victory and is therefore symbolic. Paul frequently borrows such images from then-contemporary culture, such as "leading captivity captive."

When legionnaires returned to Rome from a military conquest, they would encamp temporarily outside the city while preparations were made to celebrate the victory. Garlands were spread in the streets to overcome the odor of the filthy and sweating slaves that would march in bondage into the city. An arch was constructed through which the conquering army marched in a "ticker-tape" parade. When everything was ready, a trumpet alerted the citizens to go out and join the returning victors in the parade. The soldiers had carried into battle their banner emblazoned with the letters SPQR, which stood for the motto of the Senate and the people of Rome. Since the soldiers represented the Senate and the people, both groups were invited to join the victorious entourage.

In like manner the rapture imagery may have been designed to communicate that the people of Christ would join him in his triumphant return. The rapture imagery may be symbolic in this sense, in terms of what the rapture represents. But the rapture imagery is not symbolic in the sense that the rapture is altogether invisible.

Table 7.2

The Partial-Preterist View

A.D. 70	Still future
A coming (parousia) of Christ	The coming (parousia) of Christ
A day of the Lord	The day of the Lord
	The resurrection of the dead
	The rapture of the living
A judgment	The (final) judgment
The end of the Jewish age	The end of history

In conclusion, the chief difference between full preterists and partial preterists has to do with the *time* of the great resurrection. David Chilton (before his alleged conversion to full preterism) summed it up in the following manner: "We can add to this what the Apostle Paul tells us about the Resurrection: it will coincide with the Second Coming of Christ and the Rapture of living believers (1 Thess. 4:16–17). Some have tried to evade the force of this text by suggesting a series of resurrections—one at the Rapture, another at the Second Coming (perhaps some years later), and at least one more at the consummation of the Kingdom, the end of history (where it belongs). . . . Obviously, in terms of these texts, there can be only *one* Resurrection of believers. And this Resurrection, which coincides with the Rapture, will take place on the *Last* Day."[16]

The dispute focuses on the meaning of *the last day.* For the full preterist all references to the end and to the day of the Lord point to the destruction of Jerusalem. This is the only "second coming" or parousia of Jesus. Partial preterists make a sharp distinction between (1) the judgment-coming of Christ to the Jews at the end of the Jewish age and (2) his parousia and final coming to the world at the end of history. For the full preterist the great resurrection and the rapture occurred in the past. For the partial preterist they remain in the future.

This is the spirit of the Antichrist, which you have heard was coming, and is now already in the world.

(1 John 4:3)

8

Who Is the Antichrist?

erhaps there is no greater mystery associated with the New Testament record than the identity of the antichrist. The very mention of the word conjures up diabolical creatures such as "Rosemary's Baby," or of a human being of such unrestrained wickedness that the very mention of his name evokes terror. Futurists in eschatology regularly announce the latest candidate for the position of the antichrist. Jeane Dixon predicted that we will see the antichrist in our generation because he has already been born.

The term *antichrist* is introduced in the New Testament by the Apostle John. He speaks of the antichrist in his first epistle: "Little children, it is the last hour; and as you have heard that the Antichrist is coming, even now many antichrists have come, by which we know that it is the last hour. They went out from us, but they were not of us; for if they had been of us, they would have continued with us; but they went out that they might be made manifest, that none of them were of us. But you have an anointing from the Holy One, and you know all things." (1 John 2:18–20)

This passage includes several enigmatic elements. The first is the time-frame reference: "it is the last hour." This unique phrase is somewhat difficult to understand. We must ask the question, "This is the last hour of what?" Jesus spoke of his "hour" (Matt. 26:45), which has been interpreted to mean the hour of his death or the hour of his return to heavenly glory, both of which occurred in the first century. But here John is speaking, not of the last hour of Christ, but of the last hour of something else. Is it the last hour of the Jewish Age? Is it the last hour of world history? In other words, is it *a* last hour that has already elapsed, or is it *the* last hour of all human history?

Those who understand it to be the last hour of human history fall into two basic groups. First are biblical critics who cite this as one more example of "consistent eschatology," an eschatological expectation that failed to materialize within the predicted time-frame. Second are those who argue that "the last hour" began in New Testament times and continues to this day.

Alexander Ross says of this phrase:

> It is important to remember that, according to the New Testament, with the coming of Christ, with His Death and Resurrection and Ascension, the last period of the world's history has begun. God has spoken His final message in His Son (Heb. 1:2). No event in the world's history can ever equal in epoch-making importance the coming of Christ till He comes again. The Christian era, as it has been put, is "the last on the Divine program; the next will be the coming of the Lord." That period has lasted more than 1900 years since John wrote the words before us and it may last some time yet, but, apart from its duration, it can be thought of being, in a very real sense, the last hour. It is "the last time," as [John] Calvin says, "in which all things are so completed that nothing remains except the final revelation of Christ."[1]

To understand this approach, we must distinguish between the term *last* in this interpretation and the term *final*. Perhaps a better word to express the view of Calvin cited by Ross is that it is the "main" or "chief" redemptive-historical hour, but certainly not the "final" hour.

Whatever John means by "the last hour," he regards it as present. Twice he says it *is* the last hour. He asserts that this is certain due to the presence of the antichrist. He speaks of the antichrist in both past and future tenses. On the one hand, the antichrist *is coming*. In this case that which is coming has not yet arrived. Here John speaks of the antichrist in the singular. But then he adds, "many antichrists have come." Here antichrist is plural and already present or past. Based on the past appearances of many antichrists, John says we know that it is the last hour.

The Spirit of the Antichrist

John further qualifies his teaching regarding the antichrist:

Beloved, do not believe every spirit, but test the spirits, whether they are of God; because many false prophets have gone out into the world. By this you know the Spirit of God: Every spirit that confesses that Jesus Christ has come in the flesh is of God, and every spirit that does not confess that Jesus Christ has come in the flesh is not of God. And this is the spirit of the Antichrist, which you have heard was coming, and is now already in the world. You are of God, little children, and have overcome them, because He who is in you is greater than he who is in the world.

(1 John 4:1–4)

In this text John speaks of the *spirit* of the antichrist. His readers had heard that the antichrist *was coming*, but John says he is in the world *now* and *already*. A crucial question, however, is this: What is "already in the world"? Is it the *spirit* of the antichrist, or the antichrist himself?

To answer this question we must consider various factors. In the first place the Greek text does not include the full phrase "And this is the spirit of the Antichrist." The Greek text simply says, "And this is of the Antichrist." In the context John has been speaking of spirits that confess Christ's coming in the flesh and of spirits that deny it. John then concludes that "this is of the Antichrist." Translators add the words *the spirit* in italics to signal to the reader that they have added or supplied the words. Given the contextual discussion concerning spirits, both positive and negative, the addition of "the spirit" seems to me to be warranted.

More crucial is this question: What is the antecedent of *which* in the phrase "which you have heard was coming, and is now already in the world." Is John saying that, while the antichrist's spirit is already in the world, the antichrist himself is not yet in the world? If so, then the door is left open for a future appearance of the antichrist at the end of world history. This seems to be the view of the majority of evangelical scholars.

Another possibility is that the antichrist himself, and not merely his spirit, is already in the world during the first century. In this case, two more options surface. One is that the antichrist, though appearing in the world in the first century, has continued his activity throughout world history down to our day. This view would disqualify any human from being the antichrist unless God accorded this person miraculous longevity.

The other option is that *the* antichrist was present in the world when John wrote this epistle and the antichrist's work was limited to the first century.

Grammatically speaking, the antecedent of *which* should be "the Antichrist," not merely "the spirit of the Antichrist." If this is correct, then we must conclude that the antichrist of whom John wrote appeared in the first century.

Even if John's antichrist was a specific person in the first century, this does not preclude the possibility of other antichrists appearing at various times, or even continuously, throughout church history. This speculation gains at least some credence from John's reference to the "many antichrists" (1 John 2:18) who had preceded *the* antichrist.

Because John refers to "many antichrists," many scholars have concluded that the term *antichrist* refers not to a specific individual or a series of individuals, but to institutions or a system of teaching linked to false prophets. Some conclude that antichrist is a specific person by identifying him with "the man of lawlessness" mentioned by the Apostle Paul, or with the beast of the Book of Revelation. But neither Paul nor the Apocalypse specifically uses the term *antichrist*. Again, the only explicit references to the antichrist occur in the epistles of John.

David Chilton argues that the term *antichrist* refers both to a system of unbelief (the heresy that denied the reality of the incarnation, particularly in the manner of early Gnosticism), and to apostate individuals (like the first-century heresiarch Cerinthus). "Putting all this together," Chilton writes, "we can see that *antichrist* is a description of both *the system of apostasy* and *individual apostates.* In other words, antichrist was the fulfillment of Jesus' prophecy that a time of great apostasy would come, when 'many will fall away and will betray one another and hate one another. And many false prophets will arise, and will mislead many' (Matt. 24:10–11). . . . When the doctrine of antichrist is understood, it fits in perfectly with what the rest of the New Testament tells us about the age of the 'terminal generation.'"[2]

G. C. Berkouwer summarizes the debate by saying: "A common solution is to distinguish between 'forerunners' (antichrists) and *the* antichrist. The 'antichrists' are presently with us; the 'antichrist' will appear at the end of history. In this sense [Herman] Bavinck referred to the antichristian powers throughout history, but believed that one day these powers would be embodied in one kingdom of the world, the apotheosis of apostasy. At any rate, whether John is talking about antichrists or the antichrist, the crux of his message is a warning. The central meaning of the antichrist, according to John, is the great lie, the denial that Jesus is the Christ."[3]

Berkouwer himself rejects Bavinck's view that the antichrists are mere "forerunners." Berkouwer sees the antichrist as an alarm signal to the church of all ages. This does not answer the question, however, of whether the antichrist of whom John warned was a specific person who had appeared in the first century. John's use of the masculine singular to refer to the antichrist militates against the antichrist being a vague institution, though it does not preclude it absolutely.

Alexander Ross strongly avows that the antichrist is not an institution but a *person.* He argues this point by linking John's antichrist with Paul's "man of lawlessness," who clearly is described in personal terms. "If, as is . . . almost certainly the case,

John's Antichrist is to be identified with Paul's 'man of lawlessness' (2 Thess. 2:3)," Ross says, "the *personality* of Antichrist is clearly proved. . . . Outside the New Testament, we find writers like Justin Martyr, Irenaeus, Tertullian and Jerome dealing frequently with the subject of Antichrist, and all of these take Antichrist to be a person."[4]

The word *antichrist* is capable of more than one meaning or nuance, depending on how we understand the prefix *anti-*. The prefix normally means "against" and suggests someone who is in opposition to something. In this sense *antichrist* refers to someone who stands in opposition to Christ and who is his very antithesis. We generally use the English prefix *anti-* in the same manner to refer to someone or something that is against or in opposition to something else.

In Greek the prefix *anti-* can also be translated "in place of." That which is "anti" may function as a replacement or substitute for something. Theologians call this the *imitation motif.* So we might view the antichrist as a false Christ, or as one who seeks to usurp the rightful place of Christ. He is a fake or counterfeit Christ. Thus "imitation" refers to that which is not genuine but counterfeit.

It is not necessary to choose between these nuances of the prefix. It is possible, if not probable, that the concept of antichrist contains both elements. At the very least the antichrist is one who stands and works "against" Christ. If, however, he also seeks to be a substitute for Christ, then the link to the man of lawlessness is even more enticing.

The Man of Lawlessness

Paul introduces the man of lawlessness in his Second Epistle to the Thessalonians.

> Let no one deceive you by any means; for that Day will not come unless the falling away comes first, and the man of sin is revealed, the son of perdition, who opposes and exalts himself above all that is called God or that is worshiped, so that he sits as God in the tem-

ple of God, showing himself that he is God. Do you not remember that when I was still with you I told you these things? And now you know what is restraining, that he may be revealed in his own time. For the mystery of lawlessness is already at work; only He who now restrains will do so until He is taken out of the way. And then the lawless one will be revealed, whom the Lord will consume with the breath of His mouth and destroy with the brightness of His coming. The coming of the lawless one is according to the working of Satan, with all power, signs, and lying wonders, and with all unrighteous deception among those who perish, because they did not receive the love of the truth, that they might be saved. And for this reason God will send them strong delusion, that they should believe the lie. . . .

(2 Thess. 2:3–11)

Paul's man of sin or lawlessness is often linked to or identified with the antichrist. If indeed both names refer to the same thing, then Paul has shed considerable light on the nature and character of the antichrist. First, the man of sin is identified as a man. This would tend to eliminate institutions from being the antichrist, except when an institution can be embodied in a single individual. The Reformers commonly considered the papacy as the antichrist, an institution that could be embodied in a particular pope. Likewise some have seen the government of the Roman Empire as the antichrist, which could be embodied in a specific emperor.

Second, the man of sin's lawless behavior has a strong religious dimension. He is "the son of perdition" who not only "opposes" God but also "exalts himself above . . . God" (2 Thess. 2:3–4). Through a kind of self-apotheosis, this man claims for himself nothing short of deity. Paul does not call him "antichrist" here, but Paul does describe his activity in terms of being both *against* Christ and a *substitute* for Christ. Paul says the man of sin "sits as God in the temple of God" (2 Thess. 2:4). This suggests that this arrogant person will appear when the temple is in place, though conceivably the term *temple* merely designates a religious locale.

John Calvin, for example, had no problem seeing this as an allusion to the church. "This one word *[in the temple of God]* fully refutes the error or rather stupidity of those who hold the Pope to be the vicar of Christ on the ground that he has a settled residence in the Church, however he may conduct himself," Calvin writes. "Paul sets Antichrist in the very sanctuary of God. He is not an enemy from the outside but from the household of faith, and opposes Christ under the very name of Christ."[5]

Third, Paul comments on when the man of lawlessness will appear. Paul wrote to the Thessalonians that the "day of Christ" had not yet come. Paul said that day would not come until the apostasy (or falling away) occurs and the man of sin is revealed (2 Thess. 2:3).

What the apostle says next is the subject of great debate regarding the timing of the man of sin's appearance. Paul indicates that the "restrainer," whom his readers can identify, is present (2 Thess. 2:7). This one who restrains has been identified by modern commentators as the Roman government, Paul himself, and the Holy Spirit.

The latter is a favorite theory of some Dispensationalists who see in this text a thinly veiled reference to the rapture. That is, the rapture must occur before the antichrist is unleashed. For the antichrist to operate without restraint, the Holy Spirit must be first removed. For this to occur the Christian community must be physically removed from the earth, because as long as Christians are present in the world the Holy Spirit who indwells them is likewise present.

Whoever the restrainer is, he must be taken out of the way before the lawless one can be revealed. Paul does employ temporal terms similar to John's when he declares that "the mystery of lawlessness is *already* at work" (2 Thess. 2:7). Paul then states that "the lawless one" will be consumed by the Lord and destroyed "with the brightness of His coming" (2 Thess. 2:8). These statements imply that, though the man of lawlessness was already at work, he was not yet clearly manifest to Paul's contemporaries. This man's work would continue until Christ came and he was consumed.

Again the question of time-frame becomes critical. Was Paul speaking of a first-century person who would soon be made manifest and then be destroyed by the judgment-coming of Christ in A.D. 70? Or was Paul speaking of one who, though already at work in the first century, would not be fully revealed until sometime near the end of history as a precursor to the coming of Jesus?

Benjamin Breckinridge Warfield, cited by Gary DeMar, argues that Paul's man of lawlessness was a contemporary. Warfield writes:

> The withholding power is already present. Although the Man of Sin is not yet revealed, as a mystery his essential "lawlessness" is already working—"only until the present restrainer be removed from the midst." He expects him to sit in the "temple of God," which perhaps most naturally refers to the literal temple in Jerusalem, although the Apostle knew that the out-pouring of God's wrath on the Jews was close at hand (1 Thess. 2:16). And if we compare the description which the Apostle gives of him with our Lord's address on the Mount of Olives (Matt. 24), to which, as we have already hinted, Paul makes obvious allusion, it becomes at once in the highest degree probable that in the words, "he that exalteth himself against all that is called God, or is worshipped, so that he sitteth in the sanctuary of God showing himself that he is God," Paul can have nothing else in view than what our Lord described as "the abomination of desolation which was spoken of by Daniel the prophet, standing in the holy place" (Matt. 24:15); and this our Lord connects immediately with the beleaguering of Jerusalem (cf. Luke 21:20).[6]

DeMar argues that the apostasy of which Paul speaks (2 Thess. 2:3) was already in motion and was probably Jewish rather than Christian in nature. Paul is referring to the falling away of Jews who rejected Christ, not to an apostasy of the church at the end of history. Again DeMar quotes Warfield, who writes:

> In this interpretation, the apostasy is obviously the great apostasy of the Jews, gradually filling up all these years and hastening to its completion in their destruction. That the Apostle certainly had this rapidly completing apostasy in his mind in the severe arraign-

ment that he makes of the Jews in 1 Thess. 2:14–16, which reached its climax in the declaration that they were continually filling up more and more full the measure of their sins, until already the measure of God's wrath was prematurely . . . filled up against them and was hanging over them like some laden thunder-cloud ready to burst and overwhelm them,—adds an additional reason for supposing his reference to be to this apostasy—above all others, "the" apostasy—in this passage.[7]

In his treatment of 2 Thessalonians 2:3–11, J. B. Lightfoot identifies a clear link between John's antichrist and Paul's man of lawlessness. "One of the important features in this description is the parallel drawn between Christ and the adversary of Christ," Lightfoot writes. "Both alike are 'revealed,' and to both alike the term 'mystery' is applied. From this circumstance, and from the description given in ver. 4 of his arrogant assumption, we cannot doubt that the man of sin in St. Paul is identical with the Antichrist of St. John, the preposition in the latter term expressing the idea of antagonistic claims."[8]

The Beast

Nowhere in Scripture do we get such a graphic picture of a wicked eschatological figure as the Apocalypse provides of "the beast."

> Then I stood on the sand of the sea. And I saw a beast rising up out of the sea, having seven heads and ten horns, and on his horns ten crowns, and on his heads a blasphemous name. Now the beast which I saw was like a leopard, his feet were like the feet of a bear, and his mouth like the mouth of a lion. And the dragon gave him his power, his throne, and great authority. I saw one of his heads as if it had been mortally wounded, and his deadly wound was healed. And all the world marveled and followed the beast. So they worshiped the dragon who gave authority to the beast; and they worshiped the beast, saying, "Who is like the beast? Who is able to make war with him?" And he was given a mouth speaking great things and blasphemies, and he was given authority to continue

for forty-two months. Then he opened his mouth in blasphemy against God, to blaspheme His name, His tabernacle, and those who dwell in heaven. And it was granted to him to make war with the saints and to overcome them. And authority was given him over every tribe, tongue, and nation. And all who dwell on the earth will worship him, whose names have not been written in the Book of Life of the Lamb slain from the foundation of the world. If anyone has an ear, let him hear. He who leads into captivity shall go into captivity; he who kills with the sword must be killed with the sword. Here is the patience and the faith of the saints.

Then I saw another beast coming up out of the earth, and he had two horns like a lamb and spoke like a dragon. And he exercises all the authority of the first beast in his presence, and causes the earth and those who dwell in it to worship the first beast, whose deadly wound was healed. He performs great signs, so that he even makes fire come down from heaven on the earth in the sight of men. And he deceives those who dwell on the earth by those signs which he was granted to do in the sight of the beast, telling those who dwell on the earth to make an image to the beast who was wounded by the sword and lived. He was granted power to give breath to the image of the beast, that the image of the beast should both speak and cause as many as would not worship the image of the beast to be killed. And he causes all, both small and great, rich and poor, free and slave, to receive a mark on their right hand or on their foreheads, and that no one may buy or sell except one who has the mark or the name of the beast, or the number of his name. Here is wisdom. Let him who has understanding calculate the number of the beast, for it is the number of a man: His number is 666.

Then I looked, and behold, a Lamb standing on Mount Zion, and with Him one hundred and forty-four thousand, having His Father's name written on their foreheads. . . .

(Rev. 13:1–14:1)

Perhaps no biblical riddle has gripped and fascinated people more than this: who is the beast identified by the dreaded cryptogram 666. This riddle has fueled endless speculation throughout church history, resulting in a plethora of candidates. This person's number is referred to as "the mark of the beast."

Table 8.1

The Antichrist

Author	Description	Reference
John	As you have heard that the **Antichrist** is coming, even now many antichrists have come, by which we know that it is the last hour.	1 John 2:18
John	Every spirit that does not confess that Jesus Christ has come in the flesh is not of God. And this is the spirit of the **Antichrist**, which you have heard was coming, and is now already in the world.	1 John 4:1–4
Paul	That day will not come unless the falling way comes first, and the **man of sin** is revealed, the **son of perdition**, who opposes and exalts himself above all that is called God.	2 Thess. 2:3–4
Paul	Then the **lawless one** will be revealed. . . . The coming of the **lawless one** is according to the working of Satan, with all power, signs, and lying wonders.	2 Thess. 2:8–9
John	I saw a **beast** rising up out of the sea, having seven heads and ten horns.	Rev. 13:1
John	They worshiped the **beast**, saying, "Who is like the **beast**?". . . And he was given a mouth speaking great things and blasphemies.	Rev. 13:4–5
John	Authority was given [the **beast**] over every tribe, tongue, and nation. And all who dwell on the earth will worship him, whose names have not been written in the Book of Life.	Rev. 13:7

As "bestial" as this figure is, he is clearly identified as a human being. "In general, more attention is given to the 'riddle' of this number than to the fact that it is 'a human number,'" Berkouwer says. "In other words, that all the subhumanity of the beast is still human, proceeding from among men, and setting itself up over against God and men."[9]

Kenneth L. Gentry Jr., who has written extensively regarding the dating of the Book of Revelation,[10] has also written an entire monograph concerning the identity of the beast.[11] Gentry concurs with Berkouwer that the beast whose number is 666 is a man, which excludes demonic beings, philosophical systems, political movements or empires, or anything other than a specific, individual, human person.

Even a cursory reading of Revelation 13 makes it clear that, like the antichrist and the man of lawlessness, the beast is an extremely evil and idolatrous person. Gentry adds that, since the beast possesses great "authority" (Rev. 13:5, 7) and wears ten crowns on his head (Rev. 13:1), he must be a political figure. (This, of course, does not preclude a religious figure who, in addition to his ecclesiastical authority, is also invested with political authority. The idea of separating civil and ecclesiastical authority has not been a consistent norm throughout history.)

Gentry also argues that the "name-number" (Rev. 13:18) must speak of someone who was a *contemporary* of John's. Gentry bases this primarily on the time-frame references in the Apocalypse (which we have already examined). "This principle alone," Gentry says, "will eliminate 99.9% of the suggestions by commentators."[12]

If the beast is one of John's contemporaries, Gentry argues, then it naturally follows that it is someone *relevant* to the recipients of John's letter. This further limits the candidates for the beast.

Gentry agrees with those commentators who affirm that John's portrait of the beast shifts between generic and specific imagery. The Beast is described as having seven heads (Rev. 13:1), which indicates a collective identity such as a kingdom or empire. Yet in this same context the beast is given a specific identity associated with the cryptic number 666 (Rev. 13:18).

Gentry points out that later in Revelation the seven heads are said to represent seven mountains (Rev. 17:9):

"Here is the mind which has wisdom: The seven heads are seven mountains on which the woman sits. There are also seven kings. Five have fallen, one is, and the other has not yet come. And when he comes, he must continue a short time. And the beast that was, and is not, is himself also the eighth, and is of the seven, and is going to perdition. And the ten horns which you saw are ten kings who have received no kingdom as yet, but they receive authority for one hour as kings with the beast. These are of one mind, and they will give their power and authority to the beast."

(Rev. 17:9–13)

Some have argued that the seven-hilled city is Jerusalem, identified with Babylon because of its spiritual harlotry. The majority of commentators, however, see this as a reference to Rome, known widely as the "City on Seven Hills" or, as it was called in antiquity, the *Septimontium.*

A First-Century Candidate

With this background in mind, Gentry concludes that the beast is Lucius Domitius Ahenobarbus, more commonly known by his adoptive name, Nero.[13]

Gentry gives a synopsis of Nero's violence-studded life, including the murders of his own family members, the castration of a boy Nero "married," and the brutal murder of his pregnant wife by kicking her to death. Bizarre behavior was noted by the historian Suetonius, who wrote that Nero even "devised a kind of game, in which, covered with the skin of some wild animal, he was let loose from a cage and attacked the private parts of men and women, who were bound to stakes."[14]

Nero began his reign as emperor in A.D. 54. His imperial persecution of the Christian community was launched in A.D. 64, the same year as the famous fire that many believe was set by Nero himself. It is often assumed that the persecution of Christians, whom Nero blamed for the fire, was a diversionary tactic to shift blame for his own actions to others. Nero committed suicide in A.D. 68, when he was but 31 years of age.

Since the beast's appearance is one of the "things which must shortly take place" (Rev. 1:1), Nero is at least a *prima facie* candidate for the role of the beast. As described by ancient historians, Nero is a singularly cruel and unrestrained man of evil. Many ancient writers cite the bestial character of Nero, and Gentry summarizes these references:

> Tacitus . . . spoke of Nero's "cruel nature" that "put to death so many innocent men." Roman naturalist Pliny the Elder . . . described Nero as "the destroyer of the human race" and "the poison of the world." Roman satirist Juvenal . . . speaks of "Nero's cruel and bloody tyranny." . . . Apollonius of Tyana . . . specifically mentions that Nero was called a "beast": "In my travels, which have been wider than ever man yet accomplished, I have seen many, many wild beasts of Arabia and India; but this beast, that is commonly called a Tyrant, I know not how many heads it has, nor if it be crooked of claw, and armed with horrible fangs. . . . And of wild beasts you cannot say that they were ever known to eat their own mother, but Nero has gorged himself on this diet."[15]

In his manifestly depraved character Nero fulfilled the portrait of the beast well. The most critical question concerning Nero, however, is his relation to the number 666. In the ancient world alphabets often did double duty as a system of numbering. We are aware that Roman letters such as X, C, M, and L also functioned as numbers. Gentry notes that numerical "cryptograms" were fairly common in antiquity. "Among the Greeks," he writes, "it was called *isopsephia* ("numerical equality"); among the Jews it was called *gimatriya* ("mathematical"). Any given name could be reduced to its numerical equivalent by adding up the mathematical value of all of the letters of the name."[16]

"A *Hebrew* spelling of [Nero's] name was *Nrwn Qsr* (pronounced: Neron Kaiser)," says Gentry. "It has been documented by archaeological finds that a first century Hebrew spelling of Nero's name provides us with precisely the value of 666. [Marcus] Jastrow's lexicon of the Talmud contains this very spelling. . . . A great number of biblical scholars recognize this name as the solution to the problem. Is it not remarkable that this most relevant emperor has a name that fits precisely the required sum?"[17]

Table 8.2

Nero's Number

The numerical equivalent of one Hebrew rendering of
Nero's name, *Nrwn Qsr* (pronounced Neron Kaiser), is 666.

	Hebrew letter	*Numerical value*
N	נ	50
r	ר	200
w	ו	6
n	נ	50
Q	ק	100
s	ס	60
r	ר	200
	TOTAL	666

One fascinating aspect of this cryptogram is that a textual variant in Revelation 13:18 reads 616 rather than 666. Textual analysts ask if this variation was the result of a copyist's error or an intentional change to accommodate readers outside the scope of Revelation's initial Hebrew audience. The highly respected textual scholar Bruce M. Metzger says: "Perhaps the change was intentional, seeing that the Greek form Neron Caesar written in Hebrew characters *(nrwn qsr)* is equivalent to 666, whereas the Latin form Nero Caesar *(nrw qsr)* is equivalent to 616."[18]

It is well documented that emperor worship was practiced in first-century Rome. In A.D. 55 a statue of Nero was erected in Rome's Temple of Mars. "That Nero actually was worshiped is evident from inscriptions found in Ephesus in which he is called 'Almighty God' and 'Savior,'" Gentry notes. "Reference to Nero as 'God and Savior' is found in an inscription at Salamis, Cyprus. . . . Regarding the imperial development of the emperor cult, Caligula

(Gaius) and Nero 'abandoned all reserve' in promoting emperor worship. In fact, 'Caligula and Nero, the only two of the Julio-Claudians who were direct descendants of Augustus, demanded divine honors while they were still alive.'"[19]

What should we make of this? Many scholars view the beast in Revelation as a prophecy of a still remote future. Others see Nero as a "type" of one who has yet to be made manifest. Often the commentator's decision is governed by his view of when Revelation was written. Even if Gentry has dated Revelation correctly, that still does not exclude the possibility of a future manifestation of the beast in accord with a primary and secondary schema of prophetic fulfillment. But is such a schema necessary if the events foretold in Revelation concerned the imminent judgment of the Jewish nation and the destruction of Jerusalem?

*I saw the souls of those
who had been beheaded
for their witness to Jesus. . . .
And they lived and reigned
with Christ for a thousand years.*

(Rev. 20:4)

9

When Is the Millennium?

Ashort passage in the Book of Revelation has been the subject of vast eschatological investigation. It is the passage that speaks of a "millennium." Whole systems of eschatological thought have been labeled and identified in accordance with the place the millennium holds within each system. Eschatological views have been categorized broadly into the following schools of thought: historic premillennialism, dispensational premillennialism, amillennialism, postmillennialism, and full preterism (or realized eschatology). What follows is a brief exploration of the main tenets of these various eschatological positions, particularly with reference to the questions raised by full and partial preterism.

The text at the center of the millennium debate is Revelation 20:1–8:

> Then I saw an angel coming down from heaven, having the key to the bottomless pit and a great chain in his hand. He laid hold

of the dragon, that serpent of old, who is the Devil and Satan, and bound him for a thousand years; and he cast him into the bottomless pit, and shut him up, and set a seal on him, so that he should deceive the nations no more till the thousand years were finished. But after these things he must be released for a little while.

And I saw thrones, and they sat on them, and judgment was committed to them. And I saw the souls of those who had been beheaded for their witness to Jesus and for the word of God, who had not worshiped the beast or his image, and had not received his mark on their foreheads or on their hands. And they lived and reigned with Christ for a thousand years. But the rest of the dead did not live again until the thousand years were finished. This is the first resurrection. Blessed and holy is he who has part in the first resurrection. Over such the second death has no power, but they shall be priests of God and of Christ, and shall reign with Him a thousand years.

Now when the thousand years have expired, Satan will be released from his prison and will go out to deceive the nations which are in the four corners of the earth, Gog and Magog, to gather them together to battle, whose number is as the sand of the sea. . . .

(Rev. 20:1–8)

The standard millennial positions (each being a system of eschatology in its own right) may be summarized briefly as follows:

1. *Premillennialism* teaches that there will be a future, literal, earthly millennial kingdom, and that it will begin when Christ returns. The *pre-* indicates that Christ will return *before* the millennial kingdom is established.
2. *Amillennialism* teaches that there will be no literal millennial kingdom. The prefix *a-* indicates a simple negation.
3. *Postmillennialism* teaches that Christ will return *after (post-)* the millennial kingdom concludes.

These simple designations of *pre-*, *a-*, and *post-* help to establish the chronological relationship between the millennial kingdom and Christ's return. But in themselves they fail to capture the full measure of the alternate positions. What is in view is not simply *chronology*, but the *nature* of the kingdom of God. These positions also differ in their understanding of history, whether it be optimistic or pessimistic, and in their views of the church's strategy in fulfilling her mission. Therefore more detail regarding these various positions is necessary.

Amillennialism

Though Reformed theology is by no means monolithic regarding eschatological systems, the majority report among Reformed thinkers tends to be amillennialism. Anthony A. Hoekema describes the amillennial position:

> Amillennialists interpret the millennium mentioned in Revelation 20:4–6 as describing the present reign of the souls of deceased believers with Christ in heaven. They understand the binding of Satan mentioned in the first three verses of this chapter as being in effect during the entire period between the first and second comings of Christ....
>
> Amillennialists further hold that the kingdom of God is now present in the world as the victorious Christ is ruling his people by his Word and Spirit, though they also look forward to a future, glorious, and perfect kingdom on the new earth in the life to come.
>
> the kingdom of evil will continue to exist alongside of the kingdom of God until the end of the world.... The so-called "signs of the times" have been present in the world from the time of Christ's first coming, but they will come to a more intensified, final manifestation just before his Second Coming. The amillennialist therefore expects the bringing of the gospel to all nations and the conversion of the fulness of Israel to be completed before Christ's return. He also looks for an intensified form of tribulation and apostasy as well as for the appearance of a personal antichrist before the Second Coming.[1]

Kenneth L. Gentry Jr. cites the following features of amillennialism:

1. The church age is the kingdom era prophesied in the Old Testament, as the New Testament church becomes the Israel of God.
2. Satan was bound during Jesus' earthly ministry, restraining him while the gospel is being preached in the world.
3. Insofar as Christ presently rules in the hearts of believers, they will have some influence on culture while living out their faith.
4. Toward the end evil's growth will accelerate, culminating in the great tribulation and a personal antichrist.
5. "Christ will return to end history, resurrect and judge all men, and establish the eternal order. The eternal destiny of the redeemed may be either in heaven or in a totally renovated new earth."[2]

Dispensational Premillennialism

Dispensationalism, a relatively recent eschatological system, first appeared in the early nineteenth century in England. It has swept across the modern world, due largely to the wide influence of *The Scofield Reference Bible,* published in 1909. Dispensationalism has become in our day the majority report among evangelical Christians.

Charles Caldwell Ryrie gives the following synopsis of dispensational premillennialism:

Premillennialists believe that theirs is the historic faith of the Church. Holding to a literal interpretation of the Scriptures, they believe that the promises made to Abraham and David are unconditional and have had or will have a literal fulfillment. In no sense have these promises made to Israel been abrogated or fulfilled by the Church, which is a distinct body in this age having promises and a destiny different from Israel's. At the close of this age, premillennialists believe that Christ will return for His Church, meeting her in the air (this is not the Second Coming of Christ), which event, called the rapture or translation, will usher in a seven-year period of tribulation on the earth. After this, the Lord will return to the earth (this is the Second Coming of Christ) to establish His kingdom on the earth for a thousand years, during which time the promises to Israel will be fulfilled.[3]

Gentry summarizes the key tenets of dispensational premillennialism:

1. Christ offered to the Jews the Davidic kingdom in the first century. They rejected it, and it was postponed until the future.
2. The current church age is a "parenthesis" unknown to the Old Testament prophets.
3. God has separate programs for the church and Israel.
4. The church will ultimately lose influence in the world and become corrupted or apostate toward the end of the church age.
5. Christ will return secretly to rapture his saints before the great tribulation.
6. After the tribulation Christ will return to earth to administer a Jewish political kingdom based in Jerusalem for one thousand years. Satan will be bound, and the temple will be rebuilt and the sacrificial system reinstituted.
7. Near the end of the millennium, Satan will be released and Christ will be attacked at Jerusalem.
8. Christ will call down judgment from heaven and destroy his enemies. The (second) resurrection and the judgment of the wicked will occur, initiating the eternal order.[4]

Historic Premillennialism

Perhaps the most noted advocate of *historic premillennialism* in our day has been George Eldon Ladd. Ladd has written extensively on the subject in such works as *A Theology of the New Testament*, "Historic Premillennialism," and *The Blessed Hope.*[5] In the latter work he provides an important critique of pretribulationism (Dispensationalism) and an historical perspec-

Table 9.1

Advocates of Millennial Views

Amillennialists	Postmillennialists	
Jay E. Adams	Oswald T. Allis	J. Gresham Machen
G. C. Berkouwer	Athanasius	George C. Miladin
Louis Berkhof	Augustine	Iain H. Murray
William Hendricksen	Greg L. Bahnsen	John Murray
Anthony A. Hoekema	John Calvin	Gary North
Abraham Kuyper	Robert Lewis Dabney	John Owen
Bruce K. Waltke	John Jefferson Davis	R. J. Rushdoony
Edward J. Young	Jonathan Edwards	W. G. T. Shedd
	Eusebius	Augustus H. Strong
	A. A. Hodge	J. H. Thornwell
	Charles Hodge	B. B. Warfield
	J. Marcellus Kik	

Dispensational Premillennialists		Historical Premillennialists
Gleason L. Archer	J. Dwight Pentecost	W. J. Erdman
Donald G. Barnhouse	Charles Caldwell Ryrie	Frederic L. Godet
Lewis Sperry Chafer	John F. Walvoord	Irenaeus
J. N. Darby		Justin Martyr
M. R. DeHaan		George Eldon Ladd
Charles L. Feinberg		Papias
Norman L. Geisler		J. Barton Payne
Harry A. Ironside		Tertullian
Walter C. Kaiser		R. A. Torrey
Hal Lindsey		Theodor Zahn

tive on differences between Dispensationalism and historic premillennialism.

"The idea of a pretribulation rapture was not seen in the Scriptures by the early church fathers," Ladd argues. "They were futurists and premillennialists but not pretribulationists. This of itself indicates that pretribulationism and premillennialism are not identical and that the Blessed Hope is not the hope of a rapture before the Tribulation. Pretribulationism was an unknown teaching until the rise of the Plymouth Brethren among whom the doctrine originated. . . . The vocabulary of the Blessed Hope knows nothing of two aspects of Christ's coming, one secret and one glorious."[6]

Ladd goes on to say:

Finally, we concluded that the undue concern with the question of pretribulationism tends to cause neglect of more important and vital issues having to do with the Blessed Hope; that it is not necessary for the preservation of the purifying influence of the Blessed Hope; that it tends to misunderstand the most fundamental element in the purifying Hope; that it sacrifices one of the greatest incentives for world evangelization; that a Biblical attitude of expectancy is not identical with a belief in an any-moment coming of Christ; that it misrepresents the Blessed Hope by defining it in terms of escape from suffering rather than union with Christ and thus may be guilty of the positive danger of leaving the Church unprepared for tribulation when Antichrist appears; and that pretribulationism is not essential to a premillennial eschatology.[7]

Gentry provides a seven-point summary of historic premillennialism:

1. The New Testament era Church is the *initial* phase of Christ's kingdom, as prophesied by the Old Testament prophets.
2. The New Testament Church may win occasional victories in history, but ultimately she will fail in her mission, lose influence, and become corrupted as worldwide evil increases toward the end of the Church Age.
3. The Church will pass through a future, worldwide, unprecedented time of travail. This era is known as the Great Tribulation, which will punctuate the end of contemporary history. . . .
4. Christ will return at the end of the Tribulation to rapture the Church, resurrect deceased saints, and conduct the judgment of the righteous in the "twinkling of an eye."
5. Christ will then descend to the earth with His glorified saints, fight the battle of Armageddon, bind Satan, and establish a worldwide, political kingdom, which will be

personally administered by Him for 1,000 years from Jerusalem.

6. At the end of the millennial reign, Satan will be loosed and a massive rebellion against the kingdom and a fierce assault against Christ and His saints will occur.

7. God will intervene with fiery judgment to rescue Christ and the saints. The resurrection and the judgment of the wicked will occur and the eternal order will begin.[8]

Postmillennialism

An advocate of contemporary postmillennialism, Gentry presents several features of this view. The first is that the messianic kingdom was founded on earth during the earthly ministry of Christ in fulfillment of Old Testament prophecy. The New Testament church becomes the transformed Israel, the "Israel of God" of which Paul speaks in Galatians 6:16.

The second feature is that the kingdom is essentially redemptive and spiritual rather than political and physical.

The third feature is that the kingdom will exercise a transformational socio-cultural influence in history. Gentry quotes Greg L. Bahnsen: "The *essential distinctive* of postmillennialism is its scripturally derived, sure expectation of gospel prosperity for the church during the *present* age."[9]

The fourth feature is that the kingdom of Christ will gradually expand in time and on earth. This will be accomplished not without Christ's royal power as King but without his physical presence on earth.

The fifth feature is that the Great Commission will succeed. Gentry cites Bahnsen: "The thing that distinguishes the biblical postmillennialist, then, from amillennialists and premillennialists is his belief that the Scripture teaches *the success of the great commission in this age of the church*."[10] This expectation includes the virtual Christianization of the nations.

At this point in his summary, Gentry makes an important distinction between two types or groups of modern postmillennialists: *pietistic postmillennialists* and *theonomic postmillennialists*. The basic difference between the two has to do with the application of biblical law. "Pietistic postmillennialism (as found in Banner of Truth circles)," Gentry says, "denies that the postmillennial advance of the kingdom involves the total transformation of culture through the application of biblical law. Theonomic postmillennialism affirms this."[11]

The seventh feature is that an extended period of spiritual prosperity may endure for millennia, after which history will be drawn to a close by the personal, visible, bodily return of Christ. His return will be accompanied by a literal resurrection and a general judgment, ushering in the final and eternal form of the kingdom.

Other Differences

The differences displayed among the various millennial schools go far beyond their understanding of the millennium itself. The differences are systemic and extend to every aspect of eschatology. Some form of preterism could conceivably be incorporated into all of them. One possible exception is Dispensationalism, although with certain modifications it could fit in even there.

Partial preterism may be incorporated in both pietistic postmillennialism and theonomic postmillennialism. One need not be in the theonomic camp to embrace partial preterism. The term *theonomic* refers to a specific school of thought within contemporary Calvinism, to a specific view of the Old Testament law and its application to contemporary culture. In a broad sense all Calvinists are "theonomic," and in an even broader sense all Christians are theonomic.

The root meaning of *theonomy* is "rule by the law of God." Every Christian must, in some sense, agree that God's rule is supreme over creation. But by no means do all Christians agree with historic Calvinism that the Old Testament law has an ongoing function in the Christian life. Of Calvin's famous three-fold use of the law, the third is still hotly disputed among evangelicals. In denying the "third use" of the law, the *tertius usus,* many evangelicals, especially those within the Dispensational camp, categorically deny theonomy.

The view that the Old Testament law is not binding on the believer in any sense, a view called antinomianism, is widely held. The problem of antinomianism is a serious threat to contemporary Christianity. Over against this view all Calvinists stand together in asserting the on-going relevance and use of the Old Testament's moral law. The debate over theonomy in its narrow sense is an intramural debate among Calvinists, who agree on more regarding the Old Testament law than they disagree on. But theonomy in the narrow sense is not, as Gentry has indicated, essential to postmillennialism.

Another major difference between millennial schools is their attitudes toward the future. Postmillennialism is the most optimistic concerning the gospel's impact on history and culture. When one surveys history at the end of the twentieth century, it may seem somewhat Pollyannaish to regard the church's influence in the world with much optimism. This is especially true in light of the frequent assertion by sociologists and historians that this is the "post-Christian era." The only post-Christian era known to Scripture is eternity, which may be "post" with respect to any specific era in church history, but will certainly not be Christian. The future belongs to the people of God and to the kingdom of Christ. Some Calvinists may be pessimistic with regard to the immediate future and even with regard to the gospel's impact on culture before Christ comes again, but one cannot be a Calvinist and a pessimist about the ultimate triumph of Christ and the gospel.

Conclusion

The purpose of *The Last Days according to Jesus* has been to examine and evaluate the various claims of preterism, both full and partial. The great service preterism performs is to focus attention on two major issues. The first is the time-frame references of the New Testament regarding eschatological prophecy. The preterist is a sentinel standing guard against frivolous and superficial attempts to downplay or explain away the force of these references.

The second major issue is the destruction of Jerusalem. This event certainly spelled the end of a crucial redemptive-historical epoch. It must be viewed as the end of some age. It also represents a significant visitation of the Lord in judgment and a vitally important "day of the Lord." Whether this was the *only* day of the Lord about which Scripture speaks remains a major point of controversy among preterists.

The great weakness of full preterism—and what I regard to be its fatal flaw—is its treatment of the final resurrection. If full preterism is to gain wide credibility in our time, it must overcome this obstacle.

With respect to partial preterism, Kenneth L. Gentry Jr. has done excellent work in forcing reconsideration of the date when the Book of Revelation was written. If he is correct in arguing for a date prior to A.D. 70, then sweeping revisions must be made in our understanding of this book's content and focus.

Debates over eschatology will probably continue until the Lord returns and we have the advantage of hindsight rather than the disadvantage of foresight. The divisions that exist within the Christian community are understandable, considering that both the subject matter and the literary genre of future prophecy are exceedingly difficult. This does not mean that we may push the Bible aside or neglect its eschatological sections. On the contrary the interpretative difficulties presented by eschatological matters simply call us to a greater diligence and persistence in seeking their solution.

As I have indicated throughout this book, one of my overarching concerns regarding the points in dispute is the authority of Scripture. As the inerrant Word of God, it precludes all efforts to ignore or downplay any aspect of its teaching. The evangelical world cannot afford to turn a deaf ear to the railing voices of skepticism that gut Scripture of its divine authority, that assault the credibility of the apostolic witness and even of Christ himself. We must take seriously the skeptics' critique of the time-frame references of New Testament prophecy, and we must answer them convincingly.

Appendix 1

The Olivet Discourse
according to Matthew

Then Jesus went out and departed from the temple, and His disciples came to *Him* to show Him the buildings of the temple. And Jesus said to them, "Do you not see all these things? Assuredly, I say to you, not one stone shall be left here upon another, that shall not be thrown down."

Now as He sat on the Mount of Olives, the disciples came to Him privately, saying, "Tell us, when will these things be? And what *will be* the sign of Your coming, and of the end of the age?"

And Jesus answered and said to them:

"Take heed that no one deceives you. For many will come in My name, saying, 'I am the Christ,' and will deceive many. And you will hear of wars and rumors of wars. See that you are not troubled; for all *these things* must come to pass, but the end is not yet. For nation will rise against nation, and kingdom against kingdom. And there will be famines, pestilences, and earthquakes in various places. All these *are* the beginning of sorrows.

"Then they will deliver you up to tribulation and kill you, and you will be hated by all nations for My name's sake. And then many will be offended, will betray one another, and will hate one another. Then many false prophets will rise up and deceive many. And because lawlessness will abound, the love of many will grow cold. But he who endures to the end shall be saved. And this gospel of the kingdom will be preached in all the world as a witness to all the nations, and then the end will come.

"Therefore when you see the 'abomination of desolation,' spoken of by Daniel the prophet, standing in the holy place" (whoever reads, let him understand), "then let those who are in Judea flee to the mountains. Let him who is on the housetop not come down to take anything out of his house. And let him who is in the field not go back to get his clothes. But woe to those who are pregnant and to those with nursing babies in those days! And pray that your flight may not be in winter or on the Sabbath.

"For then there will be great tribulation, such as has not been since the beginning of the world until this time, no, nor ever shall be. And unless those days were shortened, no flesh would be saved; but for the elect's sake those days will be shortened.

"Then if anyone says to you, 'Look, here *is* the Christ!' or 'There!' do not believe *it.* For false christs and false prophets will arise and show great signs and wonders, so as to deceive, if possible, even the elect. See, I have told you beforehand. Therefore if they say to you, 'Look, He is in the desert!' do not go out; *or* Look, *He is* in the inner rooms!' do not believe *it.* For as the lightning comes from the east and flashes to the west, so also will the coming of the Son of Man be. For wherever the carcass is, there the eagles will be gathered together.

"Immediately after the tribulation of those days the sun will be darkened, and the moon will not give its light; the stars will fall from heaven, and the powers of the heavens will be shaken. Then the sign of the Son of Man will appear in heaven, and then all the tribes of the earth will mourn, and they will see the Son of Man coming on the clouds of heaven with power and great glory. And He will send His angels with a great sound of a trumpet, and they will gather together His elect from the four winds, from one end of heaven to the other.

"Now learn this parable from the fig tree: When its branch has already become tender and puts forth leaves, you know that summer *is* near. So you also, when you see all these things, know that it is near, at the *very* doors. Assuredly, I say to you, this generation will by no means pass away till all these things are fulfilled. Heaven and earth will pass away, but My words will by no means pass away.

"But of that day and hour no one knows, no, not even the angels of heaven, but My Father only. But as the days of Noah *were,* so also will the coming of the Son of Man be. For as in the days before the flood, they were eating and drinking, marrying and giving in marriage, until the day that Noah entered the ark, and did not know until the flood came and took them all away, so also will the coming of the Son of Man be. Then two *men* will be in the field: one will be taken and the other left. Two *women will be* grinding at the mill: one will be taken and the other left.

"Watch therefore, for you do not know what hour your Lord is coming. But know this, that if the master of the house had known what hour the thief would come, he would have watched and not allowed his house to be broken into. Therefore you also be ready, for the Son of Man is coming at an hour when you do not expect *Him.*

"Who then is a faithful and wise servant, whom his master made ruler over his household, to give them food in due season? Blessed *is* that servant whom his master, when he comes, will find so doing. Assuredly, I say to you that he will make him ruler over all his goods.

"But if that evil servant says in his heart, 'My master is delaying his coming,' and begins to beat *his* fellow servants, and to eat and drink with the drunkards, the master of that servant will come on a day when he is not looking for *him* and at an hour that he is not aware of, and will cut him in two and appoint *him* his portion with the hypocrites. There shall be weeping and gnashing of teeth.

"Then the kingdom of heaven shall be likened to ten virgins who took their lamps and went out to meet the bridegroom. Now five of them were wise, and five *were* foolish. Those who *were* foolish took their lamps and took no oil with them, but the wise took oil in their vessels with their lamps.

"But while the bridegroom was delayed, they all slumbered and slept. And at midnight a cry was *heard:* 'Behold, the bridegroom is coming; go out to meet him!' Then all those virgins arose and trimmed their lamps.

"And the foolish said to the wise, 'Give us *some* of your oil, for our lamps are going out.'

"But the wise answered, saying, *'No,* lest there should not be enough for us and you; but go rather to those who sell, and buy for yourselves.'

"And while they went to buy, the bridegroom came, and those who were ready went in with him to the wedding; and the door was shut. Afterward the other virgins came also, saying, 'Lord, Lord, open to us!' But he answered and said, 'Assuredly, I say to you, I do not know you.' Watch therefore, for you know neither the day nor the hour in which the Son of Man is coming.

"For the *kingdom of heaven is* like a man traveling to a far country, *who* called his own servants and delivered his goods to them. And to one he gave five talents, to another two, and to another one, to each according to his own ability; and immediately he went on a journey.

"Then he who had received the five talents went and traded with them, and made another five talents. And likewise he who *had received* two gained two more also. But he who had received one went and dug in the ground, and hid his lord's money.

"After a long time the lord of those servants came and settled accounts with them. So he who had received five talents came and brought five other talents, saying, 'Lord, you delivered to me five talents; look, I have gained five more talents besides them.'

"His lord said to him, 'Well *done,* good and faithful servant; you were faithful over a few things, I will make you ruler over many things. Enter into the joy of your lord.'

"He also who had received two talents came and said, 'Lord, you delivered to me two talents; look, I have gained two more talents besides them.'

"His lord said to him, 'Well *done,* good and faithful servant; you have been faithful over a few things, I will make you ruler over many things. Enter into the joy of your lord.'

"Then he who had received the one talent came and said, 'Lord, I knew you to be a hard man, reaping where you have not sown, and gathering where you have not scattered seed. And I was afraid, and went and hid your talent in the ground. Look, *there* you have *what is* yours.'

"But his lord answered and said to him, 'You wicked and lazy servant, you knew that I reap where I have not sown, and gather where I have not scattered seed. Therefore you ought to have deposited my money with the bankers, and at my coming I would have received back my own with interest.

"'Therefore take the talent from him, and give *it* to him who has ten talents. For to everyone who has, more will be given, and he will have abundance; but from him who does not have, even what he has will be taken away. And cast the unprofitable servant into the outer darkness. There will be weeping and gnashing of teeth.'

"When the Son of Man comes in His glory, and all the holy angels with Him, then He will sit on the throne of His glory. All the nations will be gathered before Him, and He will separate them one from another, as a shepherd divides *his* sheep from the goats. And He will set the sheep on His right hand, but the goats on the left.

"Then the King will say to those on His right hand, 'Come, you blessed of My Father, inherit the kingdom prepared for you from the foundation of the world: for I was hungry and you gave Me food; I was thirsty and you gave Me drink; I was a stranger and you took Me in; I *was* naked and you clothed Me; I was sick and you visited Me; I was in prison and you came to Me.'

"Then the righteous will answer Him, saying, 'Lord, when did we see You hungry and feed *You,* or thirsty and give *You* drink? When did we see You a stranger and take *You* in, or naked and clothe *You?* Or when did we see You sick, or in prison, and come to You?'

"And the King will answer and say to them, 'Assuredly, I say to you, inasmuch as you did *it* to one of the least of these My brethren, you did *it* to Me.'

"Then He will also say to those on the left hand, 'Depart from Me, you cursed, into the everlasting fire prepared for the devil and his angels: for I was hungry and you gave Me no food; I was thirsty and you gave Me no drink; I was a stranger and you did not take Me in, naked and you did not clothe Me, sick and in prison and you did not visit Me.'

"Then they also will answer Him, saying, 'Lord, when did we see You hungry or thirsty or a stranger or naked or sick or in prison, and did not minister to You?'

"Then He will answer them, saying, 'Assuredly, I say to you, inasmuch as you did not do *it* to one of the least of these, you did not do *it* to Me.'

"And these will go away into everlasting punishment, but the righteous into eternal life."

(Matt. 24:1–25:46)

Appendix 2

The Olivet Discourse
in Matthew, Mark, and Luke

Matthew	Mark	Luke
24:1–44	13:1–37	21:5–36
Then Jesus went out and departed from the temple, and His disciples came to Him to show Him the buildings of the temple.	Then as He went out of the temple, one of His disciples	Then, as some
	said to Him,	spoke of the temple, how it was adorned
	"Teacher, see what manner of stones and what buildings are here!"	with beautiful stones
		and donations,

Matthew	Mark	Luke
And Jesus	And Jesus answered and	He
said to them,	said to him,	said, "As for these things which
"Do you not see all these things? Assuredly, I say to you,	"Do you see these great buildings?	you see,
		the days will come in which
not one stone shall be left here upon another, that shall not be thrown down." Now as He sat on the Mount of Olives,	Not one stone shall be left upon another, that shall not be thrown down." Now as He sat on the Mount of Olives opposite the temple,	not one stone shall be left upon another that shall not be thrown down."
the disciples	Peter, James, John, and Andrew	And they
came to Him privately, saying,	asked Him privately,	asked Him, saying, "Teacher,
"Tell us, when will these things be? And what will be the sign of Your coming, and of the end of the age?"	"Tell us, when will these things be? And what will be the sign	but when will these things be? And what sign
	when all these things	will there be when these things are about
	will be fulfilled?"	to take place?"
And Jesus answered	And Jesus, answering them,	And He

Matthew	Mark	Luke
and said to them:	began to say:	said:
"Take heed that	"Take heed that	"Take heed that
no one deceives you.	no one deceives you.	you not be deceived.
For many will come	For many will come	For many will come
in My name,	in My name,	in My name,
saying,	saying,	saying,
'I am the Christ,'	'I am He,'	'I am He,'
		and, 'The time
		has drawn near.'
and will	and will	
deceive many.	deceive many.	
		Therefore
		do not go
		after them.
And you will hear	And when you hear	But when you hear
of wars and	of wars and	of wars and
rumors of wars.	rumors of wars,	commotions,
See that you		
are not troubled;	do not be troubled;	do not be terrified;
for all these things	for such things	for these things
must come to pass,	must happen,	must come to pass
		first,
but the end	but the end	but the end
is not yet.	is not yet.	will not come
		immediately."
		Then He said
		to them,
For nation will rise	For nation will rise	"Nation will rise
against nation,	against nation,	against nation,
and kingdom	and kingdom	and kingdom
against kingdom.	against kingdom	against kingdom.
And there will be	And there will be	And there will be
	earthquakes	great earthquakes
	in various places,	in various places,
	and there will be	and
famines,	famines	famines
pestilences,	and troubles.	and pestilences;
and earthquakes		
in various places.		

Matthew	Mark	Luke
		and there will be fearful sights and great signs from heaven.
All these are the beginning of sorrows.	These are the beginning of sorrows. But watch out	
		But before all these things,
	for yourselves,	
Then they will	for they will	they will lay their hands on you and persecute you,
deliver you up to tribulation and kill you,	deliver you up to councils, and you will be beaten in the synagogues.	delivering you up to the synagogues and prisons,
and you will be hated by all nations	And you will be	and you will be
	brought before rulers and kings	brought before kings and rulers
for My name's sake.	for My sake,	for My name's sake. But it will turn out for you as an occasion
	for a testimony to them.	for testimony.
And then many will be offended, will betray one another, and will hate one another. Then many false prophets will rise up		

Matthew	Mark	Luke
and deceive many. And because lawlessness will abound, the love of many will grow cold. But he who endures to the end shall be saved. And this gospel of the kingdom will be preached in all the world as a witness to all the nations, and then the end will come.	And the gospel must first be preached to all the nations.	
	But when they arrest you and deliver you up, do not worry beforehand,	
	or premeditate	Therefore settle it in your hearts not to meditate beforehand on what you
	what you will speak. But whatever is given you in that hour, speak that; for it is not you who speak, but the Holy Spirit.	will answer; for I will give you
		a mouth and wisdom which all your adversaries

Matthew	Mark	Luke
		will not be able to contradict or resist.
	Now brother will betray	You will be betrayed even by parents
	brother	and brothers, relatives and friends; and they will send some of you
	to death, and a father his child; and children will rise up against parents and cause them to be put to death.	to your death.
	And you will be hated by all men for My name's sake. But he who endures to the end	And you will be hated by all for My name's sake. But
		not a hair of your head
	shall be saved.	shall be lost. In your patience possess your souls.
Therefore when you see	But when you see	But when you see Jerusalem surrounded by armies, then know that
the 'abomination of desolation,'	the 'abomination of desolation,'	its desolation is near.

Matthew	Mark	Luke
spoken of	spoken of	
by Daniel	by Daniel	
the prophet,	the prophet,	
standing	standing	
in the holy place"	where it ought not"	
(whoever reads,		
let him	(let the reader	
understand),	understand),	
"then let those	"then let those	Then let those
who are	who are	
in Judea	in Judea	in Judea
flee to	flee to	flee to
the mountains.	the mountains.	the mountains,
Let him	And let him	let those
who is	who is	who are
on the housetop	on the housetop	in the midst
		of her
not come down	not go down	
	into the house,	
	nor enter	
to take anything	to take anything	
out of his house.	out of his house.	
		depart,
And let him	And let him	and let not those
who is	who is	who are
in the field	in the field	in the country
not go back	not go back	enter her.
to get	to get	
his clothes.	his garment.	
		For these are
		the days
		of vengeance,
		that all things
		which are written
		may be fulfilled.
But woe	But woe	But woe
to those	to those	to those
who are pregnant	who are pregnant	who are pregnant
and to those	and to those	and to those who

Matthew	Mark	Luke
nursing babies	with nursing babies	are nursing babies
in those days!	in those days!	in those days!
And pray that	And pray that	
your flight	your flight	
may not be	may not be	
in winter	in winter.	
or on the Sabbath.		
For then	For in those days	For
there will be	there will be	there will be
great tribulation,	tribulation,	great distress
such as	such as	
has not been	has not been	
since the beginning	from the beginning	
of the world	of creation	
	which God created	
until this time,	until this time,	
no, nor ever	nor ever	
shall be.	shall be.	
		in the land
		and wrath
		upon this people.
And unless	And unless	
	the Lord	
	had shortened	
those days	those days,	
were shortened,		
no flesh	no flesh	
would be saved;	would be saved.	
		And they will fall
		by the edge
		of the sword,
		and be led
		away captive
		into all nations.
but for	But for	
the elect's sake	the elect's sake,	
	whom He chose,	
	He shortened	

Matthew	Mark	Luke
those days will be shortened.	the days.	
		And Jerusalem will be trampled by Gentiles until the times of the Gentiles are fulfilled.
Then if anyone says to you, 'Look, here is the Christ!' or 'There!' do not believe it. For false christs and false prophets will arise, and show great signs and wonders, so as to deceive, if possible, even the elect.	Then if anyone says to you, 'Look, here is the Christ!' or, 'Look, He is there!' do not believe it. For false christs and false prophets will rise and show signs and wonders to deceive, if possible, even the elect. But take heed;	
See, I have told you beforehand. Therefore If they say to you, 'Look, He is in the desert!' do not go out; or 'Look, He is in the inner rooms!' do not believe it. For as the lightning	see, I have told you all things beforehand.	

Matthew	Mark	Luke
comes from the east and flashes to the west, so also will the coming of the Son of Man be. For wherever the carcass is, there the eagles will be gathered together. Immediately after the tribulation of those days	But in those days, after that tribulation,	
		And there will be signs
the sun will be darkened, and the moon will not give its light;	the sun will be darkened, and the moon will not give its light;	in the sun, in the moon, and in
the stars will fall from heaven,	the stars of heaven will fall,	the stars;
		and on the earth distress of nations, with perplexity, the sea and the waves roaring; men's hearts failing them from fear and the expectation of those things which are coming on the earth,

Matthew	Mark	Luke
and the powers	and the powers	for the powers
of the heavens	in heaven	of heaven
will be shaken.	will be shaken.	will be shaken.
Then	Then	Then
the sign of		
the Son of Man		
will appear		
in heaven, and		
then all the tribes		
of the earth		
will mourn, and		
they will see	they will see	they will see
the Son of Man	the Son of Man	the Son of Man
coming on the clouds	coming in the clouds	coming in a cloud
of heaven		
with power	with great power	with power
and great glory.	and glory.	and great glory.
And He	And then He	
will send His angels	will send His angels,	
with a great sound		
of a trumpet,		
and they will	and	
gather together	gather together	
His elect	His elect	
from the four winds,	from the four winds,	
from one end	from the farthest part	
of heaven	of earth	
to the other.	to the farthest part	
	of heaven.	
		Now when
		these things
		begin to happen,
		look up and
		lift up your heads,
		because your
		redemption
		draws near."
Now learn	Now learn	
		And He spoke

Matthew	Mark	Luke
		to them
this parable	this parable	a parable:
		"Look at
from the fig tree:	from the fig tree:	the fig tree,
		and all the trees.
When its branch	When its branch	When they
has already	has already	are already
become tender	become tender,	
and puts forth	and puts forth	budding,
leaves,	leaves,	
you	you	you see and
know	know	know for yourselves
that summer	that summer	that summer
is near.	is near.	is now near.
So you also,	So you also,	So you, likewise,
when you see	when you see	when you see
all these things,	these things	these things
	happening,	happening,
know that	know that	know that
it	it	the kingdom of God
is near,	is near,	is near.
at the very doors.	at the very doors.	
Assuredly,	Assuredly,	Assuredly,
I say to you,	I say to you,	I say to you,
this generation	this generation	this generation
will by no means	will by no means	will by no means
pass away	pass away	pass away
till all these things	till all these things	till all things
are fulfilled.	take place.	are fulfilled.
Heaven and earth	Heaven and earth	Heaven and earth
will pass away,	will pass away,	will pass away,
but My words	but My words	but My words
will by no means	will by no means	will by no means
pass away.	pass away.	pass away.
But of that	But of that	
day and hour	day and hour	
no one knows,	no one knows,	
no, not even	neither	
the angels of heaven,	the angels in heaven,	

Matthew	Mark	Luke
	nor the Son,	
but	but only	
My Father only.	the Father.	
But as the days		
of Noah were,		
so also will		
the coming		
of the Son		
of Man be.		
For as		
in the days		
before the flood,		
they were eating		
and drinking,		
marrying		
and giving		
in marriage,		
until the day		
that Noah		
entered the ark,		
and did not know		
until the flood came		
and took them		
all away,		
so also		
will the coming		
of the Son		
of Man be.		
Then two men		
will be		
in the field:		
one will be taken		
and the other left.		
Two women		
will be grinding		
at the mill:		
one will be taken		
and the other left.		
	Take heed,	But take heed

Matthew	Mark	Luke
	watch and pray; for you do not know when the time is.	
		to yourselves, lest your hearts be weighed down with carousing, drunkenness, and cares of this life, and that Day come on you unexpectedly. For it will come as a snare on all those who dwell on the face of the whole earth.
	It is like a man going to a far country, who left his house and gave authority to his servants, and to each his work, and commanded the doorkeeper to watch.	
Watch therefore, for you do not know what hour your Lord	Watch therefore, for you do not know when the master of the house	Watch therefore,

Matthew	Mark	Luke
is coming.	is coming—	
	in the evening,	
	at midnight,	
	at the crowing	
	of the rooster,	
	or in the morning	
	—lest,	
	coming suddenly,	
	he find you	
	sleeping.	
	And what I say	
	to you, I say	
	to all:	
	Watch!"	
		and pray always
		that you may be
		counted worthy
		to escape
		all these things
		that will come
		to pass,
But know this,		
that if the master		
of the house		
had known		
what hour		
the thief		
would come,		
he would		
have watched		
and not allowed		
his house		
to be broken		
into.		
Therefore		
you also		
be ready,		
		and to stand before
for the Son		the Son

Matthew	Mark	Luke
of Man is coming at an hour when you do not expect Him."		of Man."

Glossary

analogia fide. Analogy of faith; based on the principle that Scripture is its own best interpreter, this is the practice of interpreting one biblical passage in light of another. Page 66.

Apocalypse, the. The Book of Revelation.

Apocalyptic. Biblical books and passages dealing with eschatological themes; a distinct genre with many extra- biblical examples as well.

apologia. Apology, defense. Page 14.

a priori. From the former; deductively. Page 138

Consistent eschatology. The view that eschatological events are sudden, catastrophic events wrought by God, not events that evolve through evolutionary development. See pages 21, 51.

Dispensationalism. An eschatological system that sees Israel and the church as separate entities and that sees the church age being followed by Jesus' millennial reign on earth. See pages 196–97.

Eschatology. The division of systematic theology dealing primarily with the future, the last things.

explicatio ex eventu. Explication out of the event. Page 64.

Hermeneutic. A system of biblical interpretation.

hic et nunc. Here and now. Page 109.

in limine. On the threshold; at the onset. Page 67.

Olivet Discourse. Jesus' discourse to his disciples near the end of his earthly ministry. This discourse, reported in all three Synoptic Gospels but most fully in Matthew, was delivered after Jesus "sat on the Mount of Olives, opposite the temple."

Parousia. Coming; used most often of Jesus's second coming.

Pastoral Epistles. Three of Paul's letters: 1 Timothy, 2 Timothy, and Titus.

Pentateuch. The first five books of the Old Testament: Genesis, Exodus, Leviticus, Numbers, and Deuteronomy.

Preterism. An eschatological viewpoint that places many or all eschatological events in the past, especially during the destruction of Jerusalem in A.D. 70.

Full preterism assigns all of these events to the first century.

Partial preterism assigns many of these events to the first century, but not the second coming, the resurrection, and the final judgment.

Orthodox preterism is another name for partial preterism.

prima facie. At first appearance; plain or clear. Pages 17, 67, 186.

Rapture. The raising of those who are alive when the dead are resurrected.

Realized eschatology. The view that the eschatological kingdom of God was ushered in during the earthly ministry of Jesus. See page 22.

reductio ad absurdum. Reduction to the absurd. Page 61.

resurrectionis carnis. Bodily or physical resurrection. Page 159.

sensus literalis. The literary sense; the sense of a text, interpreted in light of its literary form or genre.

sola Scriptura . Scripture alone. Pages 156, 157.

Synoptic Gospels. The first three Gospels: Matthew, Mark, and Luke.

terminus ad quem. The end to which; the final limiting point. Page 38.

tertius usus. The third use (of the Law); the ongoing function of the moral law in the Christian's life. Page 202.

Notes

Introduction

1. Bertrand Russell, *Why I Am Not a Christian: And Other Essays on Religion and Related Subjects*, ed. Paul Edwards (London: Allen & Unwin / New York: Simon & Schuster, 1957), p. vi.

2. Ibid., p. vi.

3. Ibid., p. 16.

4. Ibid.

5. Ibid., pp. 16–17.

6. Adolf Harnack, *What Is Christianity? Lectures Delivered in the University of Berlin during the Winter-Term 1899–1900*, trans. Thomas Bailey Saunders, 2d ed. (1901; reprint, New York: Harper & Row, 1957).

7. Albert Schweitzer, *The Quest of the Historical Jesus: A Critical Study of Its Progress from Reimarus to Wrede*, trans. W. Montgomery (1910; reprint, New York: Macmillan, 1956).

8. Herman Ridderbos, *The Coming of the Kingdom*, trans. H. de Jongste, ed. Raymond O. Zorn (Philadelphia: Presbyterian and Reformed, 1962), p. xiii. See Johannes Weiss, *Die Predigt Jesu vom Reiche Gottes* (1892); English trans., *Jesus' Proclamation of the Kingdom of God*, ed. and trans. Richard Hyde Hiers and David Larrimore Holland, Lives of Jesus Series, ed. Leander E. Keck (Philadelphia: Fortress, 1971).

9. C. H. Dodd, *The Parables of the Kingdom* (London: Nisbet, 1935).

10. C. H. Dodd, *The Interpretation of the Fourth Gospel* (London: Cambridge University, 1953), p. 7.

11. J. Stuart Russell, *The Parousia: A Critical Inquiry into the New Testament Doctrine of Our Lord's Second Coming* (London: Daldy, Isbister,1878). New ed. (London: Unwin, 1887). Reprint of new ed.: *The Parousia: A Study of the New Testament Doctrine of Our Lord's Second Coming* (Grand Rapids: Baker, 1983).

12. Ibid., pp. 539–40.

Chapter 1, What Did Jesus Teach on Mount Olivet?

1. William L. Lane, *The Gospel according to Mark*, New International Commentary on the New Testament (Grand Rapids: Eerdmans, 1974), p. 444.

2. Vincent Taylor, *The Gospel according to St. Mark: The Greek Text with Introduction, Notes, and Indexes,* 2d ed. (1966; reprint, Grand Rapids: Baker, 1981), p. 498.

3. John Calvin, *Commentary on a Harmony of the Evangelists, Matthew, Mark, and Luke,* trans. William Pringle, vol. 3 (reprint, Grand Rapids: Baker, 1984), p. 117.

4. J. Stuart Russell, *The Parousia: A Critical Inquiry into the New Testament Doctrine of Our Lord's Second Coming,* new ed. (1887; reprint, Grand Rapids: Baker, 1983), p. 57.

5. Ibid., p. 58.

6. Ibid., p. 69. Russell cites as the source of the quotation from Josephus his *The Antiquities of the Jews,* 20.8.5–6. Whiston translates the first sentence of paragraph 5 as follows: ". . . the country was again filled with robbers and imposters, who deluded the multitude." Russell's version accurately summarizes paragraphs 5–6. See Flavius Josephus, *The Antiquities of the Jews,* in *The Works of Flavius Josephus,* trans. William Whiston, vol. 4 (reprint, Grand Rapids: Baker, 1974), p. 133 (20.8.5–6).

7. Calvin, *Commentary on a Harmony,* 3:120–21.

8. Russell, *The Parousia,* pp. 69–70.

9. W. F. Albright and C. S. Mann, *Matthew: Introduction, Translation, and Notes,* Anchor Bible, ed. W. F. Albright and David Noel Freedman (Garden City: Doubleday, 1971), p. 292.

10. Lane, *The Gospel according to Mark,* p. 458.

11. Russell, *The Parousia,* pp. 70–71.

12. Ibid., p. 71.

13. Ibid., pp. 72–73.

14. Ibid., p. 73. See Josephus, *Antiquities of the Jews,* p. 20 (18.5.3).

15. Albright and Mann, *Matthew,* p. 295.

16. Calvin, *Commentary on a Harmony,* 3:131–32.

17. Russell, *The Parousia,* pp. 75–76. Whiston's translation of the passage from Josephus: "Nor did any one of them escape with his life. A false prophet was the occasion of these people's destruction, who had made a public proclamation in the city that very day, that God commanded them to get up upon the temple, and that there they should receive miraculous signs of their deliverance." Flavius Josephus, *The Wars of the Jews,* in *The Works of Flavius Josephus,* trans. William Whiston, vol. 1 (reprint, Grand Rapids: Baker, 1974), p. 453 (6.5.2).

18. Russell, *The Parousia,* p. 77. John Peter Lange, *The Gospel according to Matthew,* trans. Philip Schaff, Commentary on the Holy Scriptures, ed. John Peter Lange (1866; reprint, Grand Rapids: Zondervan 1960), p. 428; George Campbell, *The Four Gospels Translated from the Greek: With Preliminary Dissertations, and Notes Critical and Explanatory* (Philadelphia: Bartram, 1799); and Moses Stuart [Russell does not specify the work].

19. Calvin, *Commentary on a Harmony,* 3:146.

20. A. W. Argyle, *The Gospel according to Matthew,* Cambridge Bible Commentary, ed. P. R. Ackroyd, A. R. C. Leaney, and J. W. Packer (Cambridge: Cambridge University, 1963), p. 185.

21. Russell, *The Parousia,* p. 79.

22. Ibid., p. 80. Emphasis is Russell's.

23. Ibid. Emphasis is Russell's.

24. Calvin, *Commentary on a Harmony,* 3:146.

25. Russell, *The Parousia,* pp. 81–82.

26. Ibid., p. 147.

27. Ibid., pp. 83–84.

28. Gary DeMar, *Last Days Madness: The Folly of Trying to Predict When Christ Will Return* (Brentwood, Tenn.: Wolgemuth & Hyatt, 1991), p. 122.

Chapter 2, What "Generation" Will Witness the End?

1. David Hill, *The Gospel of Matthew*, New Century Bible Commentary, ed. Ronald E. Clements and Matthew Black (London: Marshall, Morgan & Scott / Grand Rapids: Eerdmans, 1972), p. 323.

2. William L. Lane, *The Gospel according to Mark*, New International Commentary on the New Testament (Grand Rapids: Eerdmans, 1974), p. 314. See J. Schierse, *"Historische Kritik und theologische Exegese der synoptischen Evangelien erläutert an Mk. 9:1," Scholastik* 29 (1959): 520–36.

3. J. Stuart Russell, *The Parousia: A Critical Inquiry into the New Testament Doctrine of Our Lord's Second Coming*, new ed. (1887; reprint, Grand Rapids: Baker, 1983), pp. 29–30.

4. Ibid., pp. 26–27.

5. Ibid., pp. 84–85.

6. Gary DeMar, *Last Days Madness: The Folly of Trying to Predict When Christ Will Return* (Brentwood, Tenn.: Wolgemuth & Hyatt, 1991), p. 32.

7. Herman Ridderbos, *The Coming of the Kingdom*, trans. H. de Jongste, ed. Raymond O. Zorn (Philadelphia: Presbyterian and Reformed, 1962), pp. 501–502.

8. DeMar, *Last Days Madness*, pp. 33–34. The second paragraph is from A. J. Mattill Jr., *Luke and the Last Things: A Perspective for the Understanding of Lukan Thought* (Dillsboro, N.C.: Western North Carolina, 1979), p. 100.

9. DeMar, *Last Days Madness*, p. 34. David Chilton, *The Great Tribulation* (Fort Worth: Dominion, 1987), p. 3. Emphasis is Chilton's.

10. Russell, *The Parousia*, p. 85.

11. Ibid., pp. 85–87. John Peter Lange, *The Gospel according to Matthew*, trans. Philip Schaff, Commentary on the Holy Scriptures, ed. John Peter Lange (1866; reprint, Grand Rapids: Zondervan, 1960), p. 208; Rudolf Stier, *The Words of the Lord Jesus*, vol. 1, *Our Lord's First Words, and the Gospels of Matthew, Mark, and Luke Specially*, trans. William B. Pope, rev. James Strong and Henry B. Smith (New York: Tibbals, 1864), p. 207.

12. Russell, *The Parousia*, p. 87.

13. Friedrich Büchsel, *"Genea," Theological Dictionary of the New Testament*, ed. Gerhard Kittel, trans. and ed. Geoffrey W. Bromiley, vol. 1 (Grand Rapids: Eerdmans, 1964), p. 663.

14. Ibid.

15. Lane, *The Gospel according to Mark*, p. 480.

16. Ridderbos, *The Coming of the Kingdom*, p. 499. See Seakle Greijdanus, *Het heilig Evangelie naar de beschrijving van Lucas*, 2 vols., *Kommentaar op het Nieuwe Testament*, ed. Seakle Greijdanus, F. W. Grosheide, and J. A. C. van Leeuwen (Amsterdam: Van Bottenburg, 1940–41), 2:1004.

17. Ridderbos, *The Coming of the Kingdom*, p. 500.

18. Russell, *The Parousia*, pp. 54–56.

Chapter 3, What "Age" Was about to End?

1. J. Stuart Russell, *The Parousia: A Critical Inquiry into the New Testament Doctrine of Our Lord's Second Coming*, new ed. (1887; reprint, Grand Rapids: Baker, 1983), p. 23.

2. Hobart E. Freeman, *An Introduction to the Old Testament Prophets* (Chicago: Moody, 1968), pp. 145–46.

3. Ibid., p. 146.

4. Bruce Vawter, *The Conscience of Israel: Pre-exilic Prophets and Prophecy* (New York: Sheed & Ward, 1961), pp. 94–95.

5. Russell, *The Parousia*, p. 4.

6. I. Howard Marshall, *The Gospel of Luke: A Commentary on the Greek Text*, New International Greek Testament Commentary (Grand Rapids: Eerdmans, 1978), pp. 717, 719.

7. Russell, *The Parousia*, p. 39.

8. Augustus Neander, *The Life of Jesus Christ in Its Historical Connexion and Historical Developement*, 3d ed., trans. John McClintock and Charles E. Blumenthal (New York: Harper, 1849), p. 349 (§239). Quoted in Russell, *The Parousia*, p. 41.

9. Gary DeMar, *Last Days Madness: The Folly of Trying to Predict When Christ Will Return* (Brentwood, Tenn.: Wolgemuth & Hyatt, 1991), pp. 21–23.

10. Russell, *The Parousia*, pp. 197–98. In a footnote to the sentence beginning "It is sometimes said. . . ," Russell cites two sources: (1) John Peter Lange, *The Gospel according to Matthew*, trans. Philip Schaff, Commentary on the Holy Scriptures, ed. John Peter Lange (1866; reprint, Grand Rapids: Zondervan, 1960), p. 422; and (2) Henry Alford, *The Greek Testament: With a Critically Revised Text, a Digest of Various Readings, Marginal References to Verbal and Idiomatic Usage, Prolegomena, and a Critical and Exegetical Commentary*, 4th ed., 4 vols. (London: Rivingtons, 1859–61), 2:556.

Chapter 4, What Did Paul Teach in His Letters?

1. J. Stuart Russell, *The Parousia: A Critical Inquiry into the New Testament Doctrine of Our Lord's Second Coming*, new ed. (1887; reprint, Grand Rapids: Baker, 1983), p. 161.

2. John Calvin, *The Epistles of Paul the Apostle to the Romans and to the Thessalonians*, trans. Ross Mackenzie, ed. David W. Torrance and Thomas F. Torrance (Grand Rapids: Eerdmans, 1961), p. 349.

3. Jonathan Edwards, *When the Wicked Shall Have Filled Up the Measure of Their Sin, Wrath Will Come Upon Them to the Uttermost*, in *The Works of Jonathan Edwards*, ed. Edward Hickman, 2 vols. (1834; reprint, Edinburgh: Banner of Truth, 1974), 2:122.

4. Russell, *The Parousia*, p. 163.

5. Ibid., p. 192.

6. Ibid., p. 198.

7. Charles Hodge, *Commentary on the Epistle to the Romans* (1886; reprint, Grand Rapids: Eerdmans, 1950), pp. 410, 412. Emphasis is Hodge's.

8. C. K. Barrett, *A Commentary on the Epistle to the Romans*, Harper's New Testament Commentaries, ed. Henry Chadwick (New York: Harper & Brothers, 1957), pp. 252–53.

9. Russell, *The Parousia*, pp. 238–39.

10. C. Leslie Mitton, *Ephesians*, New Century Bible Commentary, ed. Ronald E. Clements and Matthew Black (London: Marshall, Morgan & Scott / Grand Rapids: Eerdmans, 1973), p. 55.

11. Russell, *The Parousia*, p. 244. W. J. Conybeare and J. S. Howson, *The Life and Epistles of St. Paul*, new ed. (1892; reprint, Grand Rapids: Eerdmans, 1953), p. 708.

12. Russell, *The Parousia*, p. 250.

13. Ibid., p. 254.

14. Simon J. Kistemaker, *Exposition of the Epistle to the Hebrews*, New Testament Commentary (Grand Rapids: Baker, 1984), p. 265.

15. Philip Edgcumbe Hughes, *A Commentary on the Epistle to the Hebrews* (Grand Rapids: Eerdmans, 1977), p. 385.

16. Ibid., p. 416.

17. Ibid., pp. 416–17. F. F. Bruce, *The Epistle to the Hebrews: The English Text with Introduction, Exposition and Notes,* New International Commentary on the New Testament, ed. F. F. Bruce (Grand Rapids: Eerdmans, 1964), p. 256. Emphasis is Bruce's.

18. Russell, *The Parousia,* p. 273.

Chapter 5, What about the Destruction of Jerusalem?

1. Franz Delitzsch, *Biblical Commentary on the Prophecies of Isaiah,* trans. James Martin, 3d ed., vol. 1 (1877; reprint, Grand Rapids: Eerdmans, 1965), p. 189.

2. See Edward J. Young, *An Introduction to the Old Testament,* rev. ed. (Grand Rapids: Eerdmans, 1960), p. 394.

3. James L. Price, *Interpreting the New Testament* (New York: Holt, Rinehart and Winston, 1961), p. 52.

4. Flavius Josephus, *The Wars of the Jews,* in *The Works of Flavius Josephus,* trans. William Whiston, 4 vols. (reprint, Grand Rapids: Baker, 1974), 1:1–521; *The Antiquities of the Jews,* in *The Works,* 2:59–4:149; *The Life of Flavius Josephus,* in *The Works,* 2:3–58; and *Against Apion,* in *The Works,* 4:151–238.

5. Price, *Interpreting the New Testament,* p. 53.

6. Josephus, *The Wars of the Jews,* 1:5 (preface, 4).

7. Ibid., 1:244 (3.7.19).

8. Ibid., 1:257–58 (3.8.3).

9. Ibid., 1:321 (4.7.3). Words in brackets supplied by Whiston.

10. Ibid., 1:382–83 (5.6.3). Whiston translates "THE STONE COMETH" as "THE SON COMETH," though he mentions the former rendering in a note.

11. J. Stuart Russell, *The Parousia: A Critical Inquiry into the New Testament Doctrine of Our Lord's Second Coming,* new ed. (1887; reprint, Grand Rapids: Baker, 1983), 1:482 (note).

12. Josephus, *The Wars of the Jews,* 1:400 (5.9.4).

13. Ibid., 1:451 (6.5.1).

14. Ibid., 1:453–54 (6.5.3).

15. Tacitus, *The Histories,* trans. Clifford H. Moore, 2 vols., Loeb Classical Library (London: Heinemann / Cambridge: Harvard University, 1931), 1:5–7 (1.2–3). Quoted in Kenneth L. Gentry Jr., *The Beast of Revelation* (Tyler, Tex.: Institute for Christian Economics, 1989), p. 72.

16. Gary DeMar, *Last Days Madness: The Folly of Trying to Predict When Christ Will Return* (Brentwood, Tenn.: Wolgemuth & Hyatt, 1991), p. 48. The two quotes are from Nigel Calder, *The Comet is Coming! The Feverish Legacy of Mr. Halley* (New York: Viking, 1980), pp. 12, 13. Tacitus, *The Annals of Imperial Rome,* ed. and trans. Michael Grant, rev. ed. (London and New York: Penguin, 1971), p. 324 (14.22); Suetonius, *The Twelve Caesars,* trans. Robert Graves rev. ed., revised by Michael Grant (London and New York: Penguin, 1979), p. 234 (6.36).

17. Josephus, *The Wars of the Jews,* 1:454 (6.5.3). Bracketed words supplied by Whiston.

18. Ibid., 1:455 (6.5.3).

19. Ibid., 1:469 (6.9.2). Bracketed words supplied by Whiston.

Chapter 6, What Did John Teach in Revelation?

1. J. Stuart Russell, *The Parousia: A Critical Inquiry into the New Testament Doctrine of Our Lord's Second Coming,* new ed. (1887; reprint, Grand Rapids: Baker, 1983), p. 366.

2. Ibid.

3. Ibid., p. 367.

4. George Eldon Ladd, *A Commentary on the Revelation of John* (Grand Rapids: Eerdmans, 1972), p. 22.

5. G. R. Beasley-Murray, ed., *The Book of Revelation*, New Century Bible Commentary, ed. Ronald E. Clements and Matthew Black (London: Marshall, Morgan, and Scott, 1974), pp. 52–53. Ernst Lohmeyer, *Die Offenbarung des Johannes*, Handbuch zum Neuen Testament, 2d ed. (Tübingen: Mohr, 1953), p. 8; and Arethas, *Echēgēseōn eis tēn Apokalupsin*, in *Catenae Graecorum patrum in Novum Testamentum*, ed. John Anthony Cramer, 8 vols. (1840; reprint, Hildesheim: Olms, 1967).

6. Robert H. Mounce, *The Book of Revelation*, New International Commentary on the New Testament, ed. F. F. Bruce (Grand Rapids: Eerdmans, 1977), pp. 64–65. See also G. B. Caird, *A Commentary on the Revelation of St. John the Divine*, Harper's New Testament Commentaries, ed. Henry Chadwick (New York: Harper & Row, 1966), p. 12.

7. Russell, *The Parousia*, p. 367.

8. Kenneth L. Gentry Jr., *Before Jerusalem Fell: Dating the Book of Revelation: An Exegetical and Historical Argument for a Pre-A.D. 70 Composition* (Tyler, Tex.: Institute for Christian Economics, 1989), p. 133. A footnote to the first sentence adds: "In addition, the present tense possibly should be so understood in Revelation 1:7; 2:5."

9. Ibid., p. 138. Walter Bauer, William F. Arndt, and F. Wilbur Gingrich, *A Greek-English Lexicon of the New Testament and Other Early Christian Literature*, 4th ed. (Chicago: University of Chicago, 1957), p. 814.

10. Joseph Henry Thayer, *A Greek-English Lexicon of the New Testament*, 4th ed. (1901; reprint, Grand Rapids: Baker, 1991), p. 616; G. Abbott-Smith, *A Manual Greek Lexicon of the New Testament*, 3d ed. (Edinburgh: T. & T. Clark, 1937), p. 441; F. J. A. Hort, *The Apocalypse of St. John 1–3: The Greek Text with Introduction, Commentary, and Additional Notes* (London: Macmillan, 1908), p. 6; Kurt Aland, *A History of Christianity*, vol. 1, *From the Beginnings to the Threshold of the Reformation*, trans. James L. Schaaf (Philadelphia: Fortress, 1985), p. 88.

11. Gentry, *Before Jerusalem Fell*, p. 141. Gentry refers to the following four works: Henry Barclay Swete, *The Apocalypse of St. John: The Greek Text with Introduction, Notes, and Indices*, 3d ed. (1922; reprint, Grand Rapids: Kregel, 1977); Albert Barnes, *Notes on the Book of Revelation*, in Albert Barnes, *Notes on the New Testament* (1884–85; reprint, Grand Rapids: Baker, 1996); Robert H. Mounce, *The Book of Revelation*, New International Commentary on the New Testament, ed. F. F. Bruce (Grand Rapids: Eerdmans, 1977), pp. 64–65; and John F. Walvoord, *The Revelation of Jesus Christ* (Chicago: Moody, 1966), pp. 35, 37.

12. Gentry, *Before Jerusalem Fell*, pp. 141–42. Thayer, *A Greek-English Lexicon, of the New Testament*, p. 396; Abbott-Smith, *A Manual Greek Lexicon*, p. 282.

13. Gentry, *Before Jerusalem Fell*, p. vi.

14. Ibid.

15. Ibid., p. 27. Quotation from Arthur S. Peake, *The Revelation of John*, Hartley Lectures (London: Joseph Johnson, 1919), p. 77.

16. Gentry, *Before Jerusalem Fell*, pp. 30–38. Gentry cites a total of 138 scholars.

17. Iranaeus, *Against Heresies*, in *The Ante-Nicene Fathers: Translations of the Writings of the Fathers down to A.D. 325*, ed. Alexander Roberts and James Donaldson, 10 vols. (reprint, Grand Rapids: Eerdmans, 1975), 1:559–60 (5.30.3). Quoted in Gentry, *Before Jerusalem Fell*, pp. 46–47.

18. F. H. Chase, "The Date of the Apocalypse: The Evidence of Irenaeus," *Journal of Theological Studies* 8 (1907): 431–32. Quoted in Gentry, *Before Jerusalem Fell*, pp. 50–51.

19. Jacobus Wettstein, *Novum Testamentum Graecum*, 2 vols. (1751–52; reprint, Graz, Austria: Akademische, 1962), 2:746; James M. Macdonald, *The Life and Writings of St. John*, ed. J. S. Howson (London: Hodder & Stoughton / New York: Scribner, Armstrong, 1877), pp. 151–72.

20. Clement of Alexandria, *The Rich Man's Salvation*, in *Clement of Alexandria*, trans. G. W. Butterworth, Loeb Classical Library (London: Heinemann / New York: Putnam's, 1919), p. 357 (par. 42). Quoted in Gentry, *Before Jerusalem Fell*, p. 68.

21. Philostratus, *The Life of Apollonius of Tyana*, 4.38. Quoted in Gentry, *Before Jerusalem Fell*, p. 70. See Philostratus, *The Life of Apollonius of Tyana, the Epistles of Apollonius and the Treatise of Eusebius*, ed. J. S. Phillimore, 2 vols. (Oxford: Oxford, 1912), 1:437–39.

22. Clement of Alexandria, *The Stromata, or Miscellanies,* in *The Ante-Nicene Fathers: Translations of the Writings of the Fathers down to* A.D. *325,* ed. Alexander Roberts and James Donaldson, 10 vols. (reprint, Grand Rapids: Eerdmans, 1975), 2:554–55 (7.17). Quoted in Gentry, *Before Jerusalem Fell*, p. 84. Emphasis is Gentry's.

23. Gentry, *Before Jerusalem Fell*, p. 109.

24. Charles C. Torrey, *The Apocalypse of John* (New Haven: Yale, 1958), p. 61. Quoted in Gentry, *Before Jerusalem Fell*, p. 151.

25. Bernhard Weiss, *A Manual of Introduction to the New Testament*, trans. A. J. K. Davidson, 2 vols., Foreign Biblical Library, ed. W. Robertson Nicoll (New York: Funk & Wagnalls, 1889), 2:82. Quoted in Gentry, *Before Jerusalem Fell*, p. 166.

26. Donald Guthrie, *New Testament Introduction*, 4th ed. (Leicester: Apollos / Downers Grove, Ill.: InterVarsity, 1990), p. 961; Mounce, *The Book of Revelation*, p. 35.

27. Gentry, *Before Jerusalem Fell*, p. 336.

Chapter 7, When Is the Resurrection?

1. Kenneth L. Gentry Jr., "A Brief Theological Analysis of Hyper-Preterism," *Chalcedon Report*, no. 384 (July 1997): 22–24; Edward E. Stevens, *Stevens' Response to Gentry: A Detailed Response to Dr. Kenneth L. Gentry Jr.'s . . ."A Brief Theological Analysis of Hyper-Preterism"* (Bradford, Penn.: Kingdom, 1997).

2. Gentry "A Brief Theological Analysis," pp. 22–23.

3. Stevens, *Stevens' Response to Gentry*, p. 2.

4. Gentry, "A Brief Theological Analysis," p. 23.

5. Stevens, *Stevens' Response to Gentry*, p. 9.

6. Ibid., p. 12. Emphasis is Stevens'.

7. Ibid., p. 1. Quotes Gentry, "A Brief Theological Analysis," p. 22.

8. J. Stuart Russell, *The Parousia: A Critical Inquiry into the New Testament Doctrine of Our Lord's Second Coming*, new ed. (1887; reprint, Grand Rapids: Baker, 1983), p. 208.

9. Ibid., p. 210.

10. Max R. King, *The Cross and the Parousia of Christ: The Two Dimensions of One Age-Changing Eschaton* (Warren, Ohio: Writing and Research Ministry, 1987), p. 410.

11. Ibid., p. 417.

12. Stevens, *Stevens' Response to Gentry*, p. 28.

13. Murray J. Harris, *Raised Immortal: Resurrection and Immortality in the New Testament* (London: Marshall Morgan & Scott, 1983 / Grand Rapids: Eerdmans, 1985); and

Harris, *From Grave to Glory: Resurrection in the New Testament: Including a Response to Norman L. Geisler* (Grand Rapids: Zondervan, 1990).

14. Russell, *The Parousia*, p. 168.

15. King, *The Cross and the Parousia of Christ*, p. 641.

16. David Chilton, *Paradise Restored: A Biblical Theology of Dominion* (Fort Worth: Dominion, 1985), p. 143.

Chapter 8, Who Is the Antichrist?

1. Alexander Ross, *The Epistles of James and John*, New International Commentary on the New Testament, ed. Ned B. Stonehouse (Grand Rapids: Eerdmans, 1954), p. 168. See also John Calvin's commentary on 1 John, and specifically his comment on 2:18; the translation is Ross's.

2. David Chilton, *Paradise Restored: A Biblical Theology of Dominion* (Fort Worth: Dominion, 1985), p. 111.

3. G. C. Berkouwer, *The Return of Christ*, trans. James Van Oosterom, Studies in Dogmatics (Grand Rapids: Eerdmans, 1972), p. 265. See Herman Bavinck, *Gereformeerde Dogmatiek*, 4th ed., 4 vols. (Kampen: Kok, 1928–30), 4:659. English translation in Bavinck, *The Last Things: Hope for This World and the Next*, ed. John Bolt, trans. John Vriend (Grand Rapids: Baker, 1996), pp. 113–14.

4. Ross, *The Epistles of James and John*, p. 169 (n. 2).

5. John Calvin, *The Epistles of Paul the Apostle to the Romans and to the Thessalonians*, trans. Ross Mackenzie, ed. David W. Torrance and Thomas F. Torrance (Grand Rapids: Eerdmans, 1961), p. 402.

6. Benjamin Breckinridge Warfield, "The Prophecies of St. Paul," in Warfield, *Biblical Doctrines* (1929; reprint, Grand Rapids: Baker, 1981), pp. 609–10. Also in Warfield, *Biblical and Theological Studies*, ed. Samuel G. Craig (Philadelphia: Presbyterian and Reformed, 1952), p. 472. Quoted in Gary DeMar, *Last Days Madness: The Folly of Trying to Predict When Christ Will Return* (Brentwood, Tenn.: Wolgemuth & Hyatt, 1991), p. 159.

7. Warfield, "The Prophecies of St. Paul" (1929), p. 612; (1952), p. 474. Quoted in Gary DeMar, *Last Days Madness*, pp. 159–60.

8. J. B. Lightfoot, *Notes on Epistles of St. Paul: 1–2 Thessalonians, 1 Corinthians 1–7, Romans 1–7, Ephesians 1:1–14*, ed. J. R. Harmer (1895; reprint, Grand Rapids: Baker, 1980), p. 111.

9. Berkouwer, *The Return of Christ*, p. 279.

10. Kenneth L. Gentry Jr., *Before Jerusalem Fell: Dating the Book of Revelation: An Exegetical and Historical Argument for a Pre-A.D. 70 Composition* (Tyler, Tex.: Institute for Christian Economics, 1989).

11. Kenneth L. Gentry Jr., *The Beast of Revelation* (Tyler, Tex.: Institute for Christian Economics, 1989).

12. Gentry, *The Beast of Revelation*, p. 10.

13. Ibid., p. 14.

14. Suetonius, *Suetonius: The Lives of the Caesars*, trans. J. C. Rolfe, 2 vols., Loeb Classical Library (Cambridge and London: Harvard University, 1914), 2:133 (6.29). Quoted in Gentry, *The Beast of Revelation*, p. 17.

15. Tacitus, *The Histories*, trans. Clifford H. Moore, 2 vols., Loeb Classical Library (London: Heinemann / Cambridge: Harvard University, 1931), 2:17, 15 (4.8,7); Pliny, *Natural History*, trans. Harris Rackham and W. H. S. Jones, 10 vols., Loeb Classical Library (London: Heinemann / Cambridge: Harvard University, 1938–63), 2:537 (7.8.46), 6:359

(22.46.92); Juvenal, *Satires*, in *Juvenal and Persius*, trans. G. G. Ramsay, rev. ed., Loeb Classical Library (Cambridge and London: Harvard University, 1940), p. 177 (8.223); Philostratus, *The Life of Apollonius of Tyana*, 4.38. Quoted in Gentry, *The Beast of Revelation*, p. 42. Cf. Philostratus, *The Life of Apollonius of Tyana, the Epistles of Apollonius and the Treatise of Eusebius*, ed. J. S. Phillimore, 2 vols. (Oxford: Oxford University, 1912), 1:437–39.

16. Gentry, *The Beast of Revelation*, p. 31.

17. Ibid., p. 34. Marcus Jastrow, ed., *A Dictionary of the Targumim, the Talmud Babli and Yerushalmi, and the Midrashic Literature*, 2 vols. (1903; reprint, New York: Pardes, 1950), 2:909.

18. Bruce M. Metzger, *A Textual Commentary on the Greek New Testament*, corrected ed. (Stuttgart: United Bible Societies, 1975), p. 750. Quoted in Gentry, *The Beast of Revelation*, p. 35.

19. Gentry, *The Beast of Revelation*, pp. 64–65.

Chapter 9, When Is the Millennium?

1. Anthony A. Hoekema, *The Bible and the Future* (Grand Rapids: Eerdmans, 1979), p. 174. Quoted in Kenneth L. Gentry Jr., *He Shall Have Dominion: A Postmillennial Eschatology* (Tyler, Tex.: Institute for Christian Economics, 1992), p. 56.

2. Gentry, *He Shall Have Dominion*, pp. 57–58.

3. Charles Caldwell Ryrie, *The Basis of the Premillennial Faith* (New York: Loizeaux, 1953), p. 12.

4. Gentry, *He Shall Have Dominion*, pp. 60–61.

5. George Eldon Ladd, *A Theology of the New Testament* (Grand Rapids: Eerdmans, 1974); "Historic Premillennialism," in Robert G. Clouse, ed., *The Meaning of the Millennium: Four Views* (Downers Grove, Ill.: InterVarsity, 1977); and *The Blessed Hope* (Grand Rapids: Eerdmans, 1956).

6. Ladd, *The Blessed Hope*, p. 162.

7. Ibid., pp. 163–64.

8. Gentry, *He Shall Have Dominion*, p. 63.

9. Greg L. Bahnsen, "The *Prima Facie* Acceptability of Postmillennialism," *Journal of Christian Reconstruction* 3 (Winter 1976–77): 66. Quoted in Gentry, *He Shall Have Dominion*, p. 71. Emphasis is Bahnsen's.

10. Bahnsen, "The *Prima Facie* Acceptability of Postmillennialism," p. 71. Quoted in Gentry, *He Shall Have Dominion*, p. 71.

11. Gentry, *He Shall Have Dominion*, p. 72. In a footnote to the reference to "Banner of Truth circles," Gentry writes: "The Calvinists who are associated with this group are self-consciously identified with the revivalistic postmillennialism of Jonathan Edwards rather than with the theonomic postmillennialism of the colonial American Puritans."

Bibliography of Works Cited

General

Abbott-Smith, G. *A Manual Greek Lexicon of the New Testament.* 3d ed. Edinburgh: T. & T. Clark, 1937.

Aland, Kurt. *A History of Christianity.* Vol. 1. *From the Beginnings to the Threshold of the Reformation.* Translated by James L. Schaaf. Philadelphia: Fortress, 1985.

Alford, Henry. *The Greek Testament: With a Critically Revised Text, a Digest of Various Readings, Marginal References to Verbal and Idiomatic Usage, Prolegomena, and a Critical and Exegetical Commentary.* 4th ed. 4 vols. London: Rivingtons, 1859–61.

Arethas. *Echēgēseōn eis tēn Apokalupsin.* In John Anthony Cramer, ed. *Catenae Graecorum patrum in Novum Testamentum.* 8 vols. 1840. Reprint ed. Hildesheim: Olms, 1967. 8:171–582.

Bahnsen, Greg L. "The *Prima Facie* Acceptability of Postmillennialism." *Journal of Christian Reconstruction* 3 (Winter 1976–77): 48–105.

Bauer, Walter, William F. Arndt, and F. Wilbur Gingrich. *A Greek-English Lexicon of the New Testament and Other Early Christian Literature.* 4th ed. Chicago: University of Chicago, 1957.

Bavinck, Herman. *Gereformeerde Dogmatiek.* 4th ed. 4 vols. Kampen: Kok, 1928–30.

————. *The Last Things: Hope for This World and the Next.* Edited by John Bolt. Translated by John Vriend. Grand Rapids: Baker, 1996.

Berkouwer, G. C. *The Return of Christ.* Translated by James Van Oosterom. Studies in Dogmatics. Grand Rapids: Eerdmans, 1972.

Büchsel, Friedrich. "*Genea.*" In Gerhard Kittel, ed. *Theological Dictionary of the New Testament.* Translated and edited by Geoffrey W. Bromiley. Vol. 1. Grand Rapids: Eerdmans, 1964. Pages 662–65.

Calder, Nigel. *The Comet Is Coming! The Feverish Legacy of Mr. Halley*. New York: Viking, 1980.

Campbell, George. *The Four Gospels Translated from the Greek: With Preliminary Dissertations, and Notes Critical and Explanatory*. Philadelphia: Bartram, 1799.

Chase, F. H. "The Date of the Apocalypse: The Evidence of Irenaeus." *Journal of Theological Studies* 8 (1907): 431–35.

Chilton, David. *The Great Tribulation*. Fort Worth: Dominion, 1987.

——————. *Paradise Restored: A Biblical Theology of Dominion*. Fort Worth: Dominion, 1985.

Clement of Alexandria. *The Rich Man's Salvation*. In *Clement of Alexandria*. Translated by G. W. Butterworth. Loeb Classical Library. London: Heinemann / New York: Putnam's, 1919. Pages 265–367.

——————. *The Stromata, or Miscellanies*. In *The Ante-Nicene Fathers: Translations of the Writings of the Fathers down to A.D. 325*. Edited by Alexander Roberts, James Donaldson, and A. Cleveland Coxe. 10 vols. Reprint ed. Grand Rapids: Eerdmans, 1975. 2: 299–568.

Conybeare, W. J., and J. S. Howson. *The Life and Epistles of St. Paul*. New ed. 1892. Reprint ed. Grand Rapids: Eerdmans, 1953.

DeMar, Gary. *Last Days Madness: The Folly of Trying to Predict When Christ Will Return*. Brentwood, Tenn.: Wolgemuth & Hyatt, 1991.

Dodd, C. H. *The Interpretation of the Fourth Gospel*. London: Cambridge University, 1953.

——————. *The Parables of the Kingdom*. London: Nisbet, 1935.

Edwards, Jonathan. *When the Wicked Shall Have Filled Up the Measure of Their Sin, Wrath Will Come upon Them to the Uttermost*. In *The Works of Jonathan Edwards*. Edited by Edward Hickman. 2 vols. 1834. Reprint ed. Edinburgh: Banner of Truth, 1974.

Freeman, Hobart E. *An Introduction to the Old Testament Prophets*. Chicago: Moody, 1968.

Gentry, Kenneth L., Jr. *The Beast of Revelation*. Tyler, Tex.: Institute for Christian Economics, 1989.

——————. *Before Jerusalem Fell: Dating the Book of Revelation: An Exegetical and Historical Argument for a Pre-A.D. 70 Composition*. Tyler, Tex.: Institute for Christian Economics, 1989.

——————. "A Brief Theological Analysis of Hyper-Preterism," *Chalcedon Report*, no. 384 (July 1997), pp. 22–24.

——————. *He Shall Have Dominion: A Postmillennial Eschatology*. Tyler, Tex.: Institute for Christian Economics, 1992.

Guthrie, Donald. *New Testament Introduction*. 4th ed. Leicester: Apollos / Downers Grove, Ill.: InterVarsity, 1990.

Harnack, Adolf. *What Is Christianity? Lectures Delivered in the University of Berlin during the Winter-Term 1899–1900*. Translated by Thomas Bailey Saunders. 2d ed. 1901. Reprint ed. New York: Harper & Row, 1957.

Harris, Murray J. *From Grave to Glory: Resurrection in the New Testament: Including a Response to Norman L. Geisler.* Grand Rapids: Zondervan, 1990.

──────. *Raised Immortal: Resurrection and Immortality in the New Testament.* London: Marshall Morgan & Scott, 1983 / Grand Rapids: Eerdmans, 1985.

Hoekema, Anthony A. *The Bible and the Future.* Grand Rapids: Eerdmans, 1979.

Iranaeus. *Against Heresies.* In *The Ante-Nicene Fathers: Translations of the Writings of the Fathers Down to A.D. 325.* Edited by Alexander Roberts and James Donaldson. 10 vols. Reprint ed. Grand Rapids: Eerdmans, 1975. 1:309–567.

Jastrow, Marcus, ed. *A Dictionary of the Targumim, the Talmud Babli and Yerushalmi, and the Midrashic Literature.* 2 vols. 1903. Reprint ed. New York: Pardes, 1950.

Josephus, Flavius. *Against Apion.* In *The Works of Flavius Josephus.* Translated by William Whiston. 4 vols. Reprint ed. Grand Rapids: Baker, 1974. 4:151–238.

──────. *The Antiquities of the Jews.* In *The Works of Flavius Josephus.* Translated by William Whiston. 4 vols. Reprint ed. Grand Rapids: Baker, 1974. 2:59–4:149.

──────. *The Life of Flavius Josephus.* In *The Works of Flavius Josephus.* Translated by William Whiston. 4 vols. Reprint ed. Grand Rapids: Baker, 1974. 2:3–58.

──────. *The Wars of the Jews.* In *The Works of Flavius Josephus.* Translated by William Whiston. 4 vols. Reprint ed. Grand Rapids: Baker, 1974. 1:1–521.

Juvenal. *Satires.* In *Juvenal and Persius.* Translated by G. G. Ramsay. Rev. ed. Loeb Classical Library. Cambridge and London: Harvard University, 1940. Pages 2–307.

King, Max R. *The Cross and the Parousia of Christ: The Two Dimensions of One Age-Changing Eschaton.* Warren, Ohio: Writing and Research Ministry, 1987.

Ladd, George Eldon. *The Blessed Hope.* Grand Rapids: Eerdmans, 1956.

──────. "Historic Premillennialism." In Robert G. Clouse, ed. *The Meaning of the Millennium: Four Views.* Downers Grove, Ill.: InterVarsity, 1977. Pages 17–40.

──────. *A Theology of the New Testament.* Grand Rapids: Eerdmans, 1974.

Macdonald, James M. *The Life and Writings of St. John.* Edited by J. S. Howson. London: Hodder & Stoughton / New York: Scribner, Armstrong, 1877.

Mattill, A. J., Jr. *Luke and the Last Things: A Perspective for the Understanding of Lukan Thought.* Dillsboro, N.C.: Western North Carolina, 1979.

Metzger, Bruce M. *A Textual Commentary on the Greek New Testament.* Corrected ed. Stuttgart: United Bible Societies, 1975.

Neander, Augustus. *The Life of Jesus Christ in Its Historical Connexion and Historical Developement.* 3d ed. Translated by John McClintock and Charles E. Blumenthal. New York: Harper, 1849.

Philostratus. *The Life of Apollonius of Tyana.* In Philostratus. *The Life of Apollonius of Tyana, the Epistles of Apollonius and the Treatise of Eusebius.* Translated by F. C. Conybeare. 2 vols. Loeb Classical Library. London: Heinemann / New York: Putnam's, 1921–27. 1:1–2:405.

Pliny. *Natural History.* Translated by Harris Rackham and W. H. S. Jones. 10 vols. Loeb Classical Library. London: Heinemann / Cambridge: Harvard University, 1938–63.

Price, James L. *Interpreting the New Testament.* New York: Holt, Rinehart and Winston, 1961.

Ridderbos, Herman. *The Coming of the Kingdom.* Translated by H. de Jongste. Edited by Raymond O. Zorn. Philadelphia: Presbyterian and Reformed, 1962.

Russell, Bertrand. *Why I Am Not a Christian: And Other Essays on Religion and Related Subjects.* Edited by Paul Edwards. London: Allen & Unwin / New York: Simon & Schuster, 1957.

Russell, J. Stuart. *The Parousia: A Critical Inquiry into the New Testament Doctrine of Our Lord's Second Coming.* New ed. 1887. Reprint ed. Grand Rapids: Baker, 1983.

Ryrie, Charles Caldwell. *The Basis of the Premillennial Faith.* New York: Loizeaux, 1953.

Schierse, J. *"Historische Kritik und theologische Exegese der synoptischen Evangelien erläutert an Mk. 9:1." Scholastik* 29 (1959): 520–36.

Schweitzer, Albert. *The Quest of the Historical Jesus: A Critical Study of Its Progress from Reimarus to Wrede.* Translated by W. Montgomery. 1910. Reprint ed. New York: Macmillan, 1956.

Stevens, Edward E. *Stevens' Response to Gentry: A Detailed Response to Dr. Kenneth L. Gentry Jr.'s . . ."A Brief Theological Analysis of Hyper-Preterism."* Bradford, Penn.: Kingdom, 1997.

Stier, Rudolf. *The Words of the Lord Jesus.* Vol. 1, *Our Lord's First Words, and the Gospels of Matthew, Mark, and Luke Specially.* Translated by William B. Pope. Revised by James Strong and Henry B. Smith. New York: Tibbals, 1864.

Suetonius. *Suetonius: The Lives of the Caesars.* Translated by J. C. Rolfe. 2 vols. Loeb Classical Library. Cambridge and London: Harvard University, 1914.

——————. *The Twelve Caesars.* Translated by Robert Graves. Rev. ed. Revised by Michael Grant. London and New York: Penguin, 1979.

Tacitus. *The Annals of Imperial Rome.* Edited and translated by Michael Grant. Rev. ed. London and New York: Penguin, 1971.

——————. *The Histories.* Translated by Clifford H. Moore. 2 vols. Loeb Classical Library. Cambridge: Harvard University / London: Heinemann, 1931.

Thayer, Joseph Henry. *A Greek-English Lexicon of the New Testament.* 4th ed. 1901. Reprint ed. Grand Rapids: Baker, 1991.

Vawter, Bruce. *The Conscience of Israel: Pre-exilic Prophets and Prophecy.* New York: Sheed & Ward, 1961.

Warfield, Benjamin Breckinridge. "The Prophecies of St. Paul." In *Biblical Doctrines.* 1929. Reprint ed. Grand Rapids: Baker, 1981. Pages 599–640. And in *Biblical and Theological Studies.* Edited by Samuel G. Craig. Philadelphia: Presbyterian and Reformed, 1952. Pages 463–502.

Weiss, Bernhard. *A Manual of Introduction to the New Testament.* Translated by A. J. K. Davidson. 2 vols. Foreign Biblical Library. Edited by W. Robertson Nicoll. New York: Funk & Wagnalls, 1889.

Weiss, Johannes. *Die Predigt Jesu vom Reiche Gottes.* 1892. English translation. *Jesus' Proclamation of the Kingdom of God.* Edited and translated by Richard Hyde Hiers and David Larrimore Holland. Lives of Jesus Series. Edited by Leander E. Keck. Philadelphia: Fortress, 1971.

Wettstein, Jacobus, ed. *Novum Testamentum Graecum.* 2 vols. 1751–52. Reprint ed. Graz, Austria: Akademische, 1962.

Young, Edward J. *An Introduction to the Old Testament.* Rev. ed. Grand Rapids: Eerdmans, 1960.

Commentaries

Isaiah

Delitzsch, Franz. *Biblical Commentary on the Prophecies of Isaiah.* Translated by James Martin. 3d ed. Vol. 1. 1877. Reprint ed. Grand Rapids: Eerdmans, 1965.

Matthew

Albright, W. F., and C. S. Mann. *Matthew: Introduction, Translation, and Notes.* Anchor Bible. Edited by W. F. Albright and David Noel Freedman. Garden City: Doubleday, 1971.

Argyle, A. W. *The Gospel according to Matthew.* Cambridge Bible Commentary. Edited by P. R. Ackroyd, A. R. C. Leaney, and J. W. Packer. Cambridge: Cambridge University, 1963.

Hill, David. *The Gospel of Matthew.* New Century Bible Commentary. Edited by Ronald E. Clements and Matthew Black. London: Marshall, Morgan & Scott / Grand Rapids: Eerdmans, 1972.

Lange, John Peter. *The Gospel according to Matthew.* Translated by Philip Schaff. Commentary on the Holy Scriptures. Edited by John Peter Lange. 1866. Reprint ed. Grand Rapids: Zondervan, 1960.

Mark

Calvin, John. *Commentary on a Harmony of the Evangelists, Matthew, Mark, and Luke.* Translated by William Pringle. Vol 3. Reprint ed. Grand Rapids: Baker, 1984.

Lane, William L. *The Gospel according to Mark.* New International Commentary on the New Testament. Grand Rapids: Eerdmans, 1974.

Taylor, Vincent. *The Gospel according to St. Mark: The Greek Text with Introduction, Notes, and Indexes.* 2d ed. 1966. Reprint ed. Grand Rapids: Baker, 1981.

Luke

Greijdanus, Seakle. *Het heilig Evangelie naar de beschrijving van Lucas.* 2 vols. *Kommentaar op het Nieuwe Testament.* Edited by Seakle Greijdanus, F. W. Grosheide, and J. A. C. van Leeuwen. Amsterdam: Van Bottenburg, 1940–41.

Marshall, I. Howard. *The Gospel of Luke: A Commentary on the Greek Text.* New International Greek Testament Commentary. Grand Rapids: Eerdmans, 1978.

Romans

Barrett, C. K. *A Commentary on the Epistle to the Romans.* Harper's New Testament Commentaries. Edited by Henry Chadwick. New York: Harper & Brothers, 1957.

Calvin, John. *The Epistles of Paul the Apostle to the Romans and to the Thessalonians.* Translated by Ross Mackenzie. Edited by David W. Torrance and Thomas F. Torrance. Grand Rapids: Eerdmans, 1961.

Hodge, Charles. *Commentary on the Epistle to the Romans.* 1886. Reprint ed. Grand Rapids: Eerdmans, 1950.

Lightfoot, J. B. *Notes on Epistles of St. Paul: 1–2 Thessalonians, 1 Corinthians 1–7, Romans 1–7, Ephesians 1:1–14.* Edited by J. R. Harmer. 1895. Reprint ed. Grand Rapids: Baker, 1980.

Ephesians

Mitton, C. Leslie. *Ephesians.* New Century Bible Commentary. Edited by Ronald E. Clements and Matthew Black. London: Marshall, Morgan & Scott / Grand Rapids: Eerdmans, 1973.

Hebrews

Bruce, F. F. *The Epistle to the Hebrews: The English Text with Introduction, Exposition and Notes.* New International Commentary on the New Testament. Edited by F. F. Bruce. Grand Rapids: Eerdmans, 1964.

Hughes, Philip Edgcumbe. *A Commentary on the Epistle to the Hebrews.* Grand Rapids: Eerdmans, 1977.

Kistemaker, Simon J. *Exposition of the Epistle to the Hebrews.* New Testament Commentary. Grand Rapids: Baker, 1984.

1 John

Calvin, John. *The Gospel according to St. John 11–21 and The First Epistle of John.* Translated by T. H. L. Parker. Calvin's Commentaries. Edited by David W. Torrance and Thomas F. Torrance. Edinburgh: Oliver and Boyd / Grand Rapids: Eerdmans, 1961.

Ross, Alexander. *The Epistles of James and John.* New International Commentary on the New Testament. Edited by Ned B. Stonehouse. Grand Rapids: Eerdmans, 1954.

Revelation

Barnes, Albert. *Notes on the Book of Revelation.* Edited by Robert Frew. In *Notes on the New Testament.* 1884–85. Reprint ed. Grand Rapids: Baker, 1996.

Beasley-Murray, G. R., ed. *The Book of Revelation.* New Century Bible Commentary. Edited by Ronald E. Clements and Matthew Black. London: Marshall, Morgan & Scott, 1974.

Caird, G. B. *A Commentary on the Revelation of St. John the Divine.* Harper's New Testament Commentaries. Edited by Henry Chadwick. New York: Harper & Row, 1966.

Hort, F. J. A. *The Apocalypse of St. John 1–3: The Greek Text with Introduction, Commentary, and Additional Notes.* London: Macmillan, 1908. Reprinted in Hort, F. J. A. *Expository and Exegetical Studies: Compendium of Works Formerly Published Separately.* Limited Classical Reprint Library. Minneapolis: Klock and Klock, 1980.

Ladd, George Eldon. *A Commentary on the Revelation of John.* Grand Rapids. Eerdmans, 1972.

Lohmeyer, Ernst. *Die Offenbarung des Johannes.* Handbuch zum Neuen Testament. 2d ed. Tübingen: Mohr, 1953.

Mounce, Robert H. *The Book of Revelation.* New International Commentary on the New Testament. Edited by F. F. Bruce. Grand Rapids: Eerdmans, 1977.

Peake, Arthur S. *The Revelation of John.* Hartley Lectures. London: Joseph Johnson, 1919.

Swete, Henry Barclay. *The Apocalypse of St. John: The Greek Text with Introduction, Notes, and Indices.* 3d ed. London: Macmillan, 1922.

Torrey, Charles C. *The Apocalypse of John.* New Haven: Yale University, 1958.

Walvoord, John F. *The Revelation of Jesus Christ: A Commentary.* Chicago: Moody, 1966.

Index of Names

Index of Scripture

R. C. Sproul is the author of *Faith Alone: The Evangelical Doctrine of Justification* and *Willing to Believe: The Controversy over Free Will*, as well as more than forty other volumes.

R. C. is founder and chairman of Ligonier Ministries, a teaching ministry that produces Christian educational materials designed to fill the gap between Sunday school and seminary. Beginning as a small study center in Ligonier, Pennsylvania, this ministry moved in 1984 to Orlando, Florida. With a staff of more than fifty people, Ligonier provides laypeople and pastors with substantive materials on theology, church history, Bible study, apologetics, and Christian ethics.

Ligonier's radio program, "Renewing Your Mind," features R. C. and is broadcast nationally, five days a week. Ligonier Ministries produces a monthly periodical, *Tabletalk*, has its own web site (see page 4 for the address), and sponsors several seminars a year, the largest of which is held in Orlando.

R. C. has taught hundreds of thousands of people through books, radio, audio and video tapes, seminars, sermons, seminary classes, and other forums. His goal is to help awaken as many people as possible to the holiness of God in all its fullness. His vision is that believers would apply truth to every sphere of their lives.

Dr. Sproul, a graduate of Westminster College, Pittsburgh Theological Seminary, and the Free University of Amsterdam, is professor of systematic theology and apologetics at Knox Theological Seminary in Fort Lauderdale and is ordained in the Presbyterian Church in America.